PURPOSE FULFILLED:

"A Guide to A Life Well Lived"

Alvin C. King

Purpose Fulfilled:
A Guide To A Life Well Lived

Copyright © 2019 Alvin C. King

Independently Published
ISBN: 978-1090592545

All rights reserved. No part of this book may be reproduced in any form or used in any manner without the written permission of the author and its publisher

Printed in the United States of America

◆ TABLE OF CONTENTS ◆

Endorsements iii
Dedication v
Foreword vii
Introduction ix
Ch 1: I'm Meant To Be (IM2B) Movement 1
Ch 2: IM2B Movement: The Principles 5
Ch 3: Chosen and Committed: IM2B Movement themes ... 21
Ch 4: The ABC's of Believing– All Believer's Choose (ABC) ... 27
Ch 5: Leadership Principles 33
Ch 6: The ABC's of Leadership: Five Principles 37
Ch 7: Professional Attributes 41
Ch 8: Limitations 43
Ch 9: Who Puts Us On Our Path To Purpose? 51
Ch 10: What Is The Pursuit of Purpose With Passion? 59
Ch 11: When Do We Accept Our Purpose? 69
Ch 12: Where Does Purpose Lead Us To or Lead Us Away From? 75
Ch 13: How Does Our Purpose Drive Us? 79
Ch 14: Why Do I Have A Purpose? 85
Ch 15: The Pursuit of Purpose, With Passion 89
About The Author 93
Acknowledgements 95

◆ ENDORSEMENTS ◆

Alvin King is a man that lives to serve others and wrote a book that illustrates that. A leader who never abuses his position of power, but instead, he acts as a liaison to better serve everyone around him. He is a family man of great character, integrity, and exemplifies the definition of a true leader.

-Ed Scott, Clemson University Hall of Fame and
ACC Basketball Legend Inductee, current coach

Alvin understands that people thrive in structure. He is very detailed and gives precise instructions while communicating to others. Leaders care about the little things and that's what he values. I am a better man and coach because I've learned these skills from him and his son Jaelen.

-Marcus Lattimore, Director of Player Development,
University of South Carolina Football

◆

I had the pleasure of being one of Alvin's Company Commanders when he was assigned as a First Sergeant. From the beginning, I was impressed with his leadership style and could tell he had a passion for guidance and mentorship. He was firm but fair to the Soldiers in our company. This guide is full of useful instruction I've seen him pass on to Soldiers throughout his career.

-Larry Shaw, MAJ, US Army, Senior Intelligence Officer

When I think of Alvin and his leadership I think of a warrior monk. Silent and wise. Not quick to make rash decisions, but rather calculated and acts only when the appropriate time strikes. These attributes don't come easy and are rarely found in leaders. I didn't serve with Alvin while in the military but I serve with him now. It would have been an honor to serve at his side and experience his leadership first hand on the battlefield.

-Steven Diaz, Purple Heart Recipient and Veteran Advocate

I had the opportunity to work alongside Alvin King at Advantage Basketball Camp. I was amazed at his ability to lead a group of individuals and create a team-oriented learning environment. He was motivational through his instruction and success was the byproduct. Not only did he show his leadership ability, but he shared his training insight in person and within this book.

-Tracy Reid, 1998 WNBA Rookie of the Year
Former WNBA player and current basketball coach

Alvin served 20 years at various echelons in the Army and had opportunities to lead at all of them. He spent six years in the Special Operations community where he had multiple combat deployments. The knowledge he obtained from the silent professionals he worked side by side with is on display here in this book. It was an honor to serve with this technical and tactical proficient leader.

-Brandon Green, CW3, Special Operations Senior Warrant Officer Advisor

◆

For the last 10 years I've known Alvin as neighbor, friend, and member of the church I pastor. What you are about to read in this book are the insights and principles that I have had a front row seat to watch in living color. Alvin doesn't just talk the talk he walks the walk.

-Randy Knechtel, Founding and Lead Pastor, Vive Church

My Brother and friend, Alvin King, is first and foremost a God-fearing man. He always displayed the utmost level of professionalism, honesty and integrity. He engaged all service members in setting realistic, measurable and attainable goals while providing the required and necessary supervision in achievement. He introduces in this book his effective and efficient leadership style through a willingness to serve all with humility and love.

He discusses how he regularly celebrated the success of others and learned from his mistakes while providing a safe environment for all to take risks and volunteer innovative recommendations. He's a man that I'll follow and give my ALL to with absolutely NO reservations.

-James Quick, Senior Targeting Advisor, CW5, US Army (retired)

◆ DEDICATION ◆

Gone, but not forgotten; a moment in time dedicated to the voices that have been laid to rest.
-Alvin King

◆

When abnormal becomes normal,

In the times of war where life and limb are lost,

Brothers in arms for the greater good, dearly pay the cost,

Sacrifice felt far and wide among family, among friends,

*All who struggle through sweat and blood
for WAR to bring an end,*

*And on the day when arms are laid down
and there is peace through land and sea,*

*The effects of war still leave their mark on those
who fought to be free,*

*Thank God whose love can heal the wounds on the body,
mind and soul,*

*Thank God for those who gave their ALL,
a gift more precious than gold!*

-Michael King

◆ FOREWORD ◆

For we are His workmanship, created in Christ Jesus for good works, which God prepared beforehand that we should walk in them.
-Ephesians 2:10

Purpose Fulfilled: A Guide to Life Well Lived is a thought-provoking title from a captivating man who strategically positions us on a comparable road that grace, mercy and understanding have traveled. A true man of value who places stock in his life journey, both the summits and valley's whilst being a husband, father, friend, and a valiant service member. This book's designation also reflects his wife and children, who have been integral in his pursuit of Purpose. The hidden and often overlooked support system that stabilizes our service members deserve their recognition and there is no denying that his family has personified and exemplified their commitment to him as well as the nation. This coupled with their unconditional and unwavering support solidifies the foundation in which the principles he has introduced and shared have been fashioned and illustrated in the pages ahead. *Webster's Dictionary* categorizes purpose as both a noun or verb since it is the reason for which something is done, how it is created or why it exists. The purpose of this book is to impact others' lives.

Thinking, "outside the box," is another way of challenging the status quo. It is evident through my interaction with First Sergeant (retired) Alvin King that he has been challenging the status quo of leadership for quite some time. Through our collaborations, he has imparted onto me how I can cultivate success by being receptive to perspectives outside of my own. I eagerly volunteered to take on this venture of providing a foreword and I was intrigued by the premise he lays out ahead. His main idea is articulated through three inquiries that he references throughout the book: what is your special gift; how do you know what it is; how do you use it?

Behold, I have given Him for a witness to the people, a leader and commander to the people.
-Isaiah 55:4

People from all walks of life can benefit from his remarkable insight and how he has defined the pursuit of purpose. Alvin is influential not only in my life but has made significant impacts on the lives of many other service members that he has encountered. Learning from his interactions is a gift you won't want to miss.

When college was no longer an option based solely on a new-found responsibility, Alvin now had a life altering decision to embrace. My initial thoughts on how he embarked on this passionate pursuit to his path spurred the following question, when did he, "Stop and Listen?" Now-a-days, many move away from talking about God, let alone putting God first in their lives. Alvin decided to examine and reflect on the terms he was given: being intentional, trusting in Him above all and how did his struggles help him understand his own process.

It was important to show this because it reflects the Alvin King that I have come to know and respect. How many of us can honestly say that we have embarked on, *a life well lived?* This is a bold statement that dared me to think and stimulate my own reflection on the following question; what have I done in my life to make such a statement?

Lastly, I am Meant To Be, I have a purpose in life and it is not too late for you to make that same affirmation. You have picked this book up and now you're almost there. Let's get started.

Semper Fi
Foreword with Honor and Respect
Lance Newman, CPI, CPS
Executive Director
Project Josiah Restoration Ministries

◆ INTRODUCTION ◆

But I consider my life of no value to myself; my Purpose is to finish my course and the ministry I received from the Lord Jesus, to testify to the gospel of God's Grace.
-Acts 20:24

What is written isn't easily articulated or merely captured as words inscribed on a piece of paper. God has bestowed an inheritance within all of us, imprinted in our DNA from birth for us to behold. He has determined our path and our interactions carefully with one another so that our Purpose align in the manner He has laid out. But is it inherent that we receive and classify His gifts as an entitlement or in contrast, do we embrace them as our very own blessing? He prepared, "the" way and now He is preparing you, daily. How do we know "the" way and more importantly when do we choose "the" way?

Now to each one the manifestation of the Spirit is given for the common good.
-1 Corinthians 12:7

You can't understand what is next for you, as it may not yet be visible. Revelations of a life worth living and a meaningful path to navigate, is something often kept from us both visually and physically. It is a mystery that may seem beyond our reach as all of us struggle against this absence in direction.

I'm now living in a season of my life nestled between reflection, (self-examination) and projection (prognostication). Working to define when and where God's Grace occurs and how I receive it.

Reflections are internal analyses, based off what and how we express ourselves. In simpler terms, the who we are or even the what we are to others. The physical form can conflict with how others perceive us. My attributes, my character, my mannerisms, my social interactions, and my economic status are just a crude measure in understanding the person I am. Are these innate characteristics that would give you a complete picture of who I am, or should they determine where I am led to in life?

The goal in life is to observe. Only then can we understand, in a self-admitted, limited way, the characteristics that define us. We attribute or project onto others, what we assume were their intentions or what we have inferred from their actions.

How many times have you heard the phrase, "What he/she said was this, but what he/she meant was this?" There is a desperate need for clarity, so people speculate and often impose their own meaning into another's mouth, thus leading them into one of their own preferable or preconceived notions of what is right. Why? As an individual would you remove yourself or your bias from the equation to avoid this influence and to mitigate your projections?

Having worked hard on listening intently, I don't infuse language with meaning unintended. Communication is only effective when it is coupled with concerted listening in order to ensure understanding. Through this, you can evaluate what has been said and decide if the opinion is relevant or based merely on an assertion.

To clarify, I am speaking about pundits or paid talking heads who litter the airways and sound waves, bleeding their opinions into the minds that they reach. They are doing us all a disservice by conjuring up thoughts that aren't consistent with our values. Any public platform should be used and respected, with a sense of obligation to speak with the intention of spreading information that is factual rather than on what is in their mind.

We all are influenced by what we hear, but the tough part lies in identifying how much weight you allot to what you hear. It's unadvisable to think that since you heard it on whatever media source you go to, it is all true. It is important to remember that the source can be part of the problem. They draw a paycheck by promoting points of view that are not solely based on facts. The thought police are to be held in contempt, as the goal of these influencers is to divide and cause dissension and isolation.

What would be the difference, or how would I vary as an influencer while attempting to share? I was not compelled by monetary reasons nor specific platforms to push an agenda. I merely was stimulated with a sense of intrigue and obliged by a need to provide guidance to others.

The guidance or instructions I wished to share were based on my time served in the Army. What I learned was hard to convey. My hope is to alert and encourage others to conduct themselves in thoughtful ways. Not an easy task or one taken on lightly.

I am proud of my time in the military and beyond that, I have an earnest sense of obligation to provide much needed guidance. I feel compelled to remind young people of living a life where Purpose serves as a guide and a way to measure their contribution and self-worth to society and their families. My eagerness to help is only matched by my commitment to recognize others who helped me and how much I feel the need to be useful to those who follow me.

I credit God above all for my survival and successes and mostly with sustaining the love and concern of my family. We all falter, but learning is always the result. And why not learn whatever you can, whenever you can. What follows is my devotion to a higher source and to share with others who might benefit from my experiences and thoughts.

I began to reflect on the reason why I chose to share my feelings with others. As a man who has been father, husband and Soldier, I have had an array of experiences throughout my life. The knowledge I have gained has had an influence on who I am and has provided me with both an awareness to what I have completed thus far and a glimpse into how far I have to go.

As a father, I have assisted in raising children that are now all out of my home and confronting life on their own terms. Each child so different from the other, yet they have elected to retain what they learned from my wife and I and now have embraced those lessons into the fabric of who they are. They each had their own special gift that we nurtured and watched mature throughout the years. It is in this way that children can be very useful to their parents. As we realize their capabilities and Purpose, we also help ourselves better understand what is truly important in life.

Through our children's growth, some things became more evident to my wife and I, and we would encourage and support their goals as best as we could. We identified that preparation is a self-paced progressive process that requires fluidity and sometimes structure can be viewed or deemed restrictive to their development. We must prepare our children for our departure which may occur at an inconvenient time if ill prepared. Growth longs to flourish during the absence of stability and dependency which can be limiting to one's transformation into responsibility and independence.

What could we do to remain relevant in our children's life skill development? We shared similarities with other parents globally. For example, when our child displayed a proclivity towards a specific talent, we took time to focus on it. We then observed it and anticipated that it would eventually exceed our expectations. Thus, we found ourselves in a place where we fell into the trap or the pitfall of desiring something more than the child themselves.

When do we step away and allow the child to figure out what they want? There are a lot of parents and children that I have met who have been victims of the same self-inflicted dilemma mentioned above. Parents will state that their child has the potential, but they fail to realize that it is just that. Parents often have trouble differentiating between what their child actually wants and what they want for their child. The fact is that reality not only interferes with a child's potential, but exposes it and enhances outside pressures to fit in. Your goals and/or regrets should not inform your expectations for another, not even your child.

We strive to lift ourselves up and to meet our own preconceived notion of success because we want to pass on our achievements to the next generations. We forget that there were struggles that we had to endure and overcome. We have learned that sheltering our kids and shielding them from struggling is good parenting. We are encouraged or better yet pressured to expect excellence and remove our children from any situation in which this excellence could be threatened. Why? Could it be that what we have passed onto our children are their inheritance of entitlement?

My hope is that through some of my insights, you will be able to answer those questions and think about what is realistic. Therefore, you can positively support your children's goals to help them grow into mature adults.

As a husband, I've learned much through my trials and mistakes. Most would not realize that more failure had occurred during the relational development with my lovely wife. Through this, we learned that we were dependent on each other's companionship and that we had to be open to someone else in order to expose our truth during this merger of two individuals into one. This is truly not as easy as it seems because we now must trust that through any incident, your spouse will be there for you and accept both your genuine successes and perceived failures.

Lastly, as a Soldier, I was privileged to serve and lead some of the greatest men and women that this country has to offer. The ideas that were shared and knowledge gained during my service were immeasurable in their value to me. This education and training that I received has assisted my development both personally and professionally.

> *Hold on to instruction, do not let it go;*
> *guard it well, for it is your life.*
> -Proverbs 4:13

If God has written "the" way, and it leaves an indelible impression or inscription on us from birth, then why do we stray off the instructed path? How do we get so far away from something that was predetermined? Is it solely defined by our choices which we would be responsible for, or can you accept a more complex reason that influences us directly?

We are the sum total of the choices we make. Simple. This statement speaks volumes to me. I can sit back and remember it being told to me by a loved one. This candid and frank declaration is profound and insightful. It explains why choices matter and how decisions have consequences that aren't easy to own.

This brings me back to reflections I have had since I've retired and what are concealed in them. How do we replicate or reproduce what is valuable and what we have seen or been introduced to today? When do we accept the challenge of our need to look back at our lives and have an honest look in the mirror? Everything is right in front of us, if only we chose to perceive, receive, and accept it into our lives. Who is the one to hold us accountable? I would state simply, that would be ourselves.

Remember that only you are you, never will that change. Let your light shine with no interruption or interference; you never know who you are supposed to be influencing, and they're depending on your light to illuminate the path.

> "Rare and precious moments, how I long to live with you eternally! If only your sweetness never ceased to touch my lips, and the flutters you evoke nevermore faded away. I dream of your arm extended immeasurably to keep hold of my reaching hand. But Father Time, being a cruel master, will not grant such a wish. And so, I tuck you away as cherished memories, stored in a treasure box buried in my heart. And in times of solitude, I shall bring you out to view like rainbows." -Richelle E. Goodrich, *Making Wishes*

We must combine our precious moments with our appreciation of deliberate time management to learn how to be both efficient and effective with our activities. We must create a platform where others can do the same. How do we do so?

I'm Meant To Be (IM2B) Movement

*Not by accident nor by chance,
Sculpted am I by my Maker's hands,
For I am Meant To Be*
-Michael King

Merriam Webster defines a movement as, "a group of people working together to advance their shared political, social, or artistic ideas."

The I'm Meant To Be Movement (IM2B) was based on the foundation that everyone has a Purpose, everyone needs a Purpose to succeed, and that everyone's Purpose was given to them with hopes that they share it with others for the greater good.

Why did I decide to title it the way I did? There was a sense of responsibility that I recognized and felt compelled to act upon. Especially now in our culture that has something absent, something that we all have seemed to move away from at some point or another. Based upon my own life and what I have been exposed to, I would say that we all have an issue today with Purpose.

What I mean by this is that I believe there are a few things we are overlooking individually. In doing this, we deny owning our talents or our purpose because they don't seem applicable to us. We all have a God given gift. This is an undeniable fact. We are all born to complete a part of the bigger puzzle and play an essential role in our time here on earth.

I found this relevant as I went through life and was introduced to so many things through my travels and experience. I understood if we simplified our viewpoint, then we would get back to realizing our true potential. I know it wasn't until later in my life that my passion became more evident with the clarity of a veil being lifted from in front of my eyes. I could now see it and in turn live it.

As much as I strayed or deviated from the path, it was still there and anxiously waiting for me to accept and then embark on my journey with it, time and again. I had to learn to make things easier, I had to learn to slow down and understand that there was meaning in every moment, and if I failed to advance with cautious steps, then I would miss out on something that was accessible although it wasn't *visible* to me at that moment.

When life is at its purest form, are we not in an unassuming or docile state? We begin to confuse "stuff" with value. We begin to inject what we like, want or even need into the equation. But what is the result of such thinking? To covet, and that often results in poor choices.

Are we not complete and in our natural form when we are born? And as a child, do we not remain innocent or oblivious to what others find essential? We become preoccupied with so much and we are moved, or I would even propose "displaced" from our path, by a need to acquire "things" that disrupt (or interfere) with us recognizing our path.

> *But when Jesus saw it, he was indignant and said to them, "Let the children come to me; do not hinder them, for to such belongs the kingdom of God."*
> *-Mark 10:14*

It is clear, without hindrance and interference, that the Kingdom of God would be open to all. Do we not long to be a part of something? Do we not have an innate sense or an uncontrollable desire that draws us to be communal?

I want you to know and understand this statement. I'm Meant To Be. Say it out loud to yourself now. Now that you've said it out loud, think about it. I'm Meant To Be, it is just that unassuming. That I'm supposed to be here and that I have meaning.

Even the letters in the acronym (IM2B) – I would like you to read them out loud. Letter by letter. I M 2 B. I am to be, is a mantra, you can say repetitively. You can pass this message on to your friends and family. It's a proclamation that you can share and that you can accept as true.

To me, it was very easy to settle on this phrasing because it was easy to remember and repeat. You could see it on a sign, a bumper sticker or even on a t-shirt. We are in a time where we are all inundated with choices to decipher what is right from wrong, the left from the right, and even our value as people.

These choices should not be what motivates us daily. We should be resolute in recognizing our importance. We should be refreshed, renewed, and reinforced frequently by our resolve. We should want to track down our path with the same dedication that our path is persistently moving towards us.

Your means of existence longs for you to find it, longs for you to accept it, longs for you to understand it, and finally, it desires for you to share it. And in that process, self-awareness and Purpose meet.

As a young, teenage, college dropout who had no sense of direction and a new-found responsibility, – parenthood, I found myself in this place where I had to choose who I wanted to be moving forward. In search of an answer, I struggled through failure which hovered around me with a sense of inevitability. This course that was laid out in front of me required my full attention. To behave like a grown up and accept life as a challenge unknowable yet designed to provide useful instruction.

Was I honestly equipped for this journey or better yet; was I equal to the task? If not, could I formulate a plan along the way. My steps were illuminated for me; but was I drawn to the light at this time? Every successful expedition requires a foundation that you can feel committed to. Now was the time for me to take a firm grasp of the rudder and begin to navigate my way through life. That would necessitate me to have values, directives, or a set of better instructions that would guide me and align with whatever concerns I might have about the path before me.

IM2B MOVEMENT: THE PRINCIPLES

This crossroad in life is where the movement was birthed, and it became apparent that I must manifest a need to incur waypoints and to acknowledge requirements necessary for each stage in my life. There are five core and fundamental principles in the IM2B Movement that I wish to introduce.

    I. Aspire to Inspire
   II. Believe to Achieve
  III. Live on Purpose
  IV. Live with Purpose
   V. Trust the Process

ASPIRE TO INSPIRE

I started with Aspire to Inspire, which is a challenge. I hope that every day you should wake up, aspiring to inspire others through your actions. I believe self-examination could be useful for us to endure on our path every day. We should accept and embark on a self-guided tour of introspection daily. This tour gives us reason and is more like an injunction to us to move forward in a thoughtful way.

Every day you should try to be the best you, that you can be, and in turn, others would be motivated to do the same. Through your behavior, they will see an illustration of how to conduct themselves and they will want to duplicate that. It is the great multiplier of what we all need. Simply put, if we wake up and test ourselves, then greatness follows, or at a minimum lends us all a much-needed assist.

My father introduced me to the *Serenity Prayer*. I was very young, and this remembrance was unusual in that unlike most early memories, this one stuck with me. It was in a small, dark room, filled with strangers from all walks of life. These men and women shared one thing, they were broken.

But they were refreshed and renewed as they stood in unison and recited this prayer at the conclusion of their evening. A night filled with tales, adventures and lifetime experiences that were brutal and graphic. But those memories that they released and shared were theirs and were a unique part in their life narrative.

No one could take their involvement in mischief away and no one could live as they did. What these speeches or talks did was bring them all to a place of recovery, a place of hope. This hope was felt throughout the whole room. I always wondered how hopeful they were when they left and were outside of the comfort of this safe desolate room they now assembled in as a collective. Did they feel comforted and absolved or just a sense of relief?

The words of the prayer fascinated me, and I was drawn into a conclusion very early, that choice was a very perilous thing. Choice was a loaded word, full of numerous connotations and if left unguarded it could have serious consequences. As a young child, I read it over and over as I walked around the house. I heard it in our family conversations. I was mesmerized in a way by the simplicity, or the straightforwardness of the message, and frankly it baffles me how others could so easily discard such a simple message of absolution and help.

> *"God, grant me the serenity to accept the things*
> *I cannot change, Courage to change the things I can*
> *and Wisdom to know the difference."*
> *-Reinhold Niebuhr*

Serenity is defined by *Merriam Webster* as, "The state of being calm, peaceful, and untroubled." Asking God for peace in your life is very broad but having peace of mind to accept things you cannot change is different.

Remaining calm under pressure was a key for achievement that I incorporated and valued most while serving in the military. When deployed I would spend time contemplating as a leader, what separated me from those I lead. Was it only my rank or position based on my years within the military? This burden was ever present. I would reflect on each situation and conclude that the pressure to fulfill my responsibilities as a Soldier conflicted with concerns for the absence that I felt for loved ones left behind. The separation is felt acutely on both sides and isn't easily tolerated.

I can think of story after story where I was afforded an opportunity to remain calm and provide clear and concise directions under direct and indirect stress. I honestly think that using my people skills was something I cherished. I could relate to people in a meaningful way and meet people where they were in life at that moment. I learned that trusting my gut and instincts helped me immeasurably in getting past what lay ahead.

I always went back to, control who and what you can in that moment, because each instant should never be taken for granted or dismissed. To expedite something has its attraction and can be vital for triumph in many walks of life, but not always an easy or safe way to accomplish goals.

Understanding that you cannot impact change or that you lack control is paramount to your future successes. Otherwise you're doomed to fall into the same traps or troubles, destined to repeat history.

> *"The definition of insanity is doing the same thing over and over again but expecting different results."*
> -Albert Einstein

In my military experiences I was more in control when I was at peace, even in the face of a storm. Training can only prepare and simulate but so much. When you're faced with the authenticity of the sounds, the smells and the emotions of war, you soon realize that your expectations did not begin to approximate the reality on the ground.

As a leader you're expected to walk the walk, talk the talk and concurrently show those who depend on you what right looks like. I've been through countless hours of training and leadership development, but to me, there was a secret to my leadership style and achievements. Peace and serenity.

How could you not allow your emotions to take over? This is not always as easy as it sounds. Loss of control in a setting that changes instantly can materialize abruptly and within a moment's notice. Threats are all around, both in and outside the wire. You're on edge at every minute and oddly enough, it is here that you begin to normalize this situation. You can capture your serenity and here alone is where you are, with your brothers and sisters in a foreign land, waiting on the unexpected and the truly incomprehensible.

We have emotions that are equally tied to our actions and decisions. I have had many times where I've had to step away and not permit my fundamental or instinctive frame of mind to influence or impress upon my judgment. But, can I honestly say that I went through my career or even my life trying to achieve that kind of level headedness? Absolutely not, not even close, but I strove to do so and held myself accountable when I came up short.

I know failure intimately, and the truth is, "I will fail again," was the thought going through my mind as I observed Soldiers who found themselves in trouble. Their decisions led them to places where they should not be and as a leader, you're faced with both the consequence and the results of their actions.

I remember an incident where I failed while deployed as a junior leader. Through my irresponsibility, I showed my Command that I still had time for development. I remember exactly what I was told by my Commander. He took me outside and as we sauntered along the fence line he leaned in and asked me, *"Are you a screw up or have you just screwed up?"* It was at this instant that I knew this was a test of both my professional skills and my ability to lead. I was disappointed in myself because I had not accomplished what was expected of me. I was blessed to have another chance. This opening motivated me and fixated me on being mindful of my goals. It drove me to be better because the truth was, falling short of expectations could have grave consequences, and that Soldiers lives were dependent upon me being a better leader.

I took my management role as all other leaders do, very seriously. I was charged with leading, coaching, training, and mentoring the future leaders of the Army. The Army as an organization has a system of bottom up development of supervisory training.

We all must start at the bottom, (or close to it), to then earn our way up the ladder like our civilian contemporaries in some sense, but so different in many other respects. In the military, I would tell my Soldiers, that you cannot be fired. The reality is that you can be dismissed to an extent. My reason behind this was to illustrate that you cannot be fired if you accept that you're meant to be where you are now in this instant. In turn, you must embrace your challenges to advance because that is what you're expected to do. Move forward.

In all career fields, interactions are personality driven and this can produce a contentious work environment. I would advise Soldiers on the differences between military service and civilian work are not as dissimilar as you would think. To me, the common denominator is people. The truth is that we will have to deal with people in both career tracks. If you were running away from people or personalities, then you would be running a long time. I would highlight the prospects that they had and were afforded in the armed service, but it was their choice to decide to commit.

If you think commitment is hard, then you will probably elect to move on from the military. I would just remind them that moving on was not equivalent to failure of any sort or disappointment. We all have our own route we must follow. Discontent is an issue we must move past, but we seem to diminish the value of failure or even avoid examining what we think is failure. Why? Should you be defined by failure? What is failure?

Failure should not be an ending, but a beginning. It is through failure that we learn more about our limits, our methods or our approach to certain tasks. We only know through doing what is and what is not possible. Success and failure are not to be exclusively viewed as a destination and should never be regarded as such. Success and failure are all a part of your process, they are essential for growth. You cannot have progress without tension or a struggle, you cannot have loss without an attempt or an effort.

Consider this when you deliberate about failure and how it contributes to your own development. Do you not need to stress your muscles for growth? Do you need to challenge them until they almost fail, for them to cultivate or to increase their stamina? In the Army we continue to train in excess. To me we performed this way because your life is full of diminishing or perishable skills. Without the proper time dedicated to development, you are destined to be ill prepared.

As a group, there were baseline tasks that all Soldiers were obliged to complete. When they did, they would then be pushed further. We increased stressful situations to simulate the hardships of combat. The truth is, we could never accurately replicate the feelings, the noises, the adrenaline, and the sensory overload, but you can activate their insight on the unknown and they would profit from training for a multitude of possibilities.

As a leader, I would like to say, that I aimed to motivate my Soldiers through my example. Somedays, I fell short, but I picked myself back up and learned valuable lessons that I took forward in the aspects of my evolving towards growth and professionalism. It was a challenge that drove me every day. This is something that you not only have to know and feel, but you must also believe.

BELIEVE TO ACHIEVE

I am an advocate for the concept that any act we complete is internalized. I have a strong belief that every action must be understood, and every thought must be learned by you before you can justly realize the reason for the things you are called upon to perform.

Belief cannot be overlooked or mistaken for anything else. Understanding the reason and replicating it provides you with comprehension. What I'm saying is that, you cannot be loved unless you first love yourself. Using love as my example, we must delve into this. How can I truly love someone, if I don't love myself?

Love is something that happens immediately, within the first second of your life. You are given unconditional love by those around you, because you cannot care for yourself. Love is an emotion that we absorb, and it develops in many forms, shapes and expressions.

As a child, I didn't comprehend why my parents separated. Was there an event or even an occasion or incident that I was a part of that led to cause this? Was it my fault? Did one's love for me outweigh the others? These are questions I asked myself at a very young age. I was very inquisitive and was not a child easily pacified. So, this separation that occurred would have to be clarified, but unfortunately it never was entirely. Sadly, the causes were eventually revealed, and I knew then that it wasn't me and that I must now learn to accept this as my new normal.

I had a lot of development that I went through at an early age because I had to absorb what love was, what was meant by it, how to love, and why to love. I had to be able to comprehend and rationalize this feeling before I could replicate and reciprocate it unto someone else. Oddly enough, I think as an older sibling I was able to learn unconditional love from my younger sister.

She remains one of my heroes because of her strength and the graceful way she approached life. We often wish, pray and even hope that sickness gets better because in that instant we are too weak to understand the why. Conversely as such a young child with an insurmountable illness in her life, she was still all heart. She would take time to console you and to share her time with you. She was thoughtful and kind in her actions.

I often wondered how, how it was possible for someone so young to be so balanced and so resilient. Most would remark that she was an old soul after their exchanges with her. She enjoyed her moment, as brief as it may have been. She smiled. She loved. She relished her time that she was blessed to have. Her behavior through adversity were ones that even now as an adult I struggle with and wonder why that's so. Her smile remains in my mind because through her pain and suffering she maintained her smile.

How do we learn to replicate? This goes with any deed; how could I expect to honestly respect someone if I never respected myself? How could I expect honesty from my partner or anyone, if I'm not first honest with myself? I can think of example after example. The truth is, we have a few things that guide us as people and they all must work concurrently, but sometimes they all are demanding our time and our attention. This can produce emotional conflict.

There is a focus in your life that should be first and foremost and that is you need to get yourself together. Learn to accept you for you, learn to be okay with you, learn to appreciate that you have a reason to be here and that you cannot complete that when you're not focused. You must start with yourself; learn, grasp, and understand what your "why" is and does, this way you can mirror it with others.

It is that unassertive. Credibility is the key that we have confidence in one another. But, how do you know what to accept as true? What does certainty look like? Is there a belief class or an acceptance book you can read that will enhance your, "how to," or your, "know how?"

If you claim, (state or assert that something is the case, typically without providing evidence or proof), something or you proclaim, (declare something one considers important with due emphasis) something, does that mean that you acknowledged and accepted it as truth, or you've substantiated its validity? You cannot make an assertion and pass it off as fact.

Let's take the first premise if you claim belief, that specifically does not confirm credibility. This claim is baseless without some sort of act or some sort of additional documents or proof. How do we get to the other side of trusting? How do we get to the solution at the end of this equation?

Striving towards self-awareness helps you develop and mature. You must possess an understanding that you and only you control your feelings and views. You must be very deliberate in your process to remain on your track.

A proclamation is accentuated through an act. You have this declaration that you have confidence in and through this certainty you are now driven. This determination should carry you to your accomplishment, it is a physical component that now surfaces and continues to fuel you throughout the process.

Live ON Purpose

Which leads me to, Live ON Purpose. What does it mean, to Live ON Purpose? This is a way of life that demands an intentional attitude and confidence. I would say that it is a deliberate choice to live this way. You would be exact in your manner and explicit in your actions.

When we put God first, we will not be surprised in what our outcome or results are. But determination alone would not get you through the day, you must couple that with a direction and combine it all together with passion or a hunger for it.

There is a challenge in the Serenity Prayer about finding the courage to change the things you can. You would need to accept and illustrate this courage that will assist you in being more intentional in your actions and to be the change agent in things you would like to see.

To give you an example, I set my alarm and wake up ON Purpose daily. This is a deliberate activity. I was intentionally setting myself off on a course that requires me to complete a specific action or task. My Purpose. Another way of expressing this is a habit loop that reinforces, encourages and promotes discipline.

I usually combine the third and fourth principles when I share this message, Living ON and WITH Purpose. The emphasis to me is key in my perceived difference between the ON and WITH Purpose phrasing.

Living ON Purpose; can you answer that you really live ON Purpose? Do you relish every minute you have? We are usually not as appreciative of the struggles we survive, and we typically overlook our successes or maybe even marginalize them.

We have a common characterization of accomplishment that limits our imagination, so we can miss out on what we are here for specifically. Meaningful living requires us to fulfill our goals and we all must be flexible yet exact with our intentions. For example, you ever notice when you know it is something that you're not supposed to be doing, that you begin to ask more questions, (both to yourself and to others), or think about alternative reasons to justify why you're going to do it anyway. Careless thinking that can lead you astray is only a reality through your choices.

Focusing on the third principle enables us to wake up day-to-day, in search of our ambition. That quest is what should promote determination, it should fuel us with aim and stimulate our minds with positivity. We should want to be certain, though doubt may intrude that we can attain anything we are required to, and towards that end it makes clear, "our why."

LIVE WITH PURPOSE

Living WITH Purpose, is a culmination of acceptance, understanding, and your effort in your application. We all have a reason why we are here. We all need that cause to focus on. Once we have recognized this, we must couple this with a direction and with motivation, so we can complete any task ahead. I learned from the Army that within the definition of leadership that purpose, direction and motivation were a necessity.

Therefore, I assert that the definition of Army Leadership ties all of that together. We need to break the "with" Purpose down by each required act. How do you agree to accomplish something? How do you comprehend something? How do you share with someone?

When you accept this idea as certainty, what is the root of the veracity or the origin of the truth in that acceptance? Was it merely a list of information, or was it based on an interaction and something learned?

> *For we are His workmanship, created in*
> *Christ Jesus for good works, which God*
> *prepared beforehand, that we should walk in them.*
> *-Ephesians 2:10*

We are equipped before we even get here. We have been crafted, our book written, and our pathway laid out. Now, we must learn to follow our heart and not be controlled or misled by our power of choice. We have been endowed with a map, a goal, a destination to reach, but inevitably we all get there at different times in our lives.

What gets in the way? I would answer without hesitation, us. We are our own worst enemies, we allow doubt and external influences or disturbances to change our pursuits. What if we could get out of our own way?

How nice would it be to live with the goals we are supposed to be aware of because they are configured for us? This is the fight, the struggle, the battle we have with ourselves regularly. When you're cognizant of how it was chosen and recognized, then you're now heading towards fulfillment which can lead to a life worth living.

We must display resolve, be resolute, and to be quite honest, we must accept the challenge that life throws at us without any hesitations or conditions. To devote our talents to our determination, we can begin to see that we are moving forward, we can see that progress is achievable.

Trust the Process

As cliché as it sounds, it is something I've been saying for years to groups of Soldiers and Leaders, youth groups, and basically anyone who would listen. We must trust that we are on our right track. We must have conviction or commitment in our pursuits. We must trust that we have devotion and possess a spirit that not only connects but directs us in life.

I heard a gentleman once say, *youth is wasted on the young.* I know this seems so random or trivial, but it stuck with me. If we take the five principles and tie them together, then we will realize where we are and what we are supposed to be; then how can we not be successful?

The issue lies in the fact that we are too young to receive and recognize things and that wisdom is only gained through time and experience. So, the wasted youth in my mind does not speak to the physical, but it speaks to our intellect and the necessary knowledge base that affects the acts we need to employ and information we need to obtain.

How many of us are willing to trust the process? Are we quick to relinquish control to others? Trusting the process is truly a culmination of what I was trying to accomplish with these five principles and this list was beneficial in my own life and evolution as a leader.

If we look back at them, you can see how these five life ideologies could assist you in finding, accepting, acknowledging, and sharing your Purpose.

We must first start within. If we challenge ourselves to be better each day, then we can be a light for others. So, to me, we are all destined to be leaders. Everyone's leadership style will be different, but the truth is that we all must lead others because that is what we are required to do.

As someone in charge, you must have confidence in yourself as well as others. You must learn to echo this feeling and trust in your self-worth and enable others to be certain of themselves. If you didn't believe in someone, would you follow them? Take some time to reflect on that question, if yes was the answer you settled on, then I have a follow up question. Why?

Humans are sentient beings, by this I mean they are endowed with a need to fulfill self-actualization or goals that help us recognize our predetermined destination. They maintain a sense of urgency through what is often unclear, yet it propels them forward continuously.

> *"Ours not to reason why, ours but to do and die."*
> -Alfred Lord Tennyson

As a Soldier and as a person in authority we tie this simple statement to our reasoning. We must be certain of our leaders without fail or hesitation. Questioning an order is tricky as it supposes that you know as much as the person issuing the order. Alternative options can be successful and yield unexpected results but are also highly risky as they are based on intuition which can lead you astray.

We should not question an order, we should follow an order to complete the mission. Unfortunately, we all have one thing in common, choice. You can choose not to listen or accept it as a truth, that is your choice.

I was taught early on in my supervisory position, that you should never bring your management a problem, you should bring them a variety of solutions. Be a resolution focused leader was what I took away from my initial training. There is no one right way, but there are many right ways. The difference between your right and my right, is our interpretation.

How does a person locate themselves or better find their drive when the information and guidance we receive is often contradictory, lacking in logic, and not devoid of emotion which is such a strong human motivator?

I would say as a leader you have to have humility and acknowledge that humbleness isn't a sign of complacency, but rather it is a symbol of mindfulness that corresponds to you and your team's effort. Modesty teaches us to be cautious and thoughtful and is beneficial to survival. That means that you base your decisions on orders combined with experiences and encounters, and these involvements can play a significant role in influencing your conclusions.

The fact is, things are fluid, and they change constantly. Recognition and acceptance of this fluidity helps our minds to move forward as we must be flexible and eager to adapt to whatever we encounter. Our connections and affiliations are loosely based on the time of day. While inconsistent this tension helps us realize being highly adaptable in positions of authority tends to engender confidence in the leader and in turn the subordinate is more likely to respect your ability to lead.

These are lofty goals that may seem insurmountable, yet it can result in your being more effective. This is something that you must recognize even in the face of adversity. Greatness comes in many forms and rarely does it have anything to do with material acquisitions. Greatness is an intimidating term and can cause one to feel defeated. In this regard, your heart plays a crucial role because when you give selflessly, you feel it as it derives from a higher source expressing pleasure. And so you enjoy the benefit from the glow of light and hope that this pleasure provides.

"It is human nature to think wisely and act foolishly."
-Anatole France

Chosen and Committed: IM2B Movement Themes

For many are called, but few are chosen.
-Matthew 22:14

Chosen ◆

What better way to jumpstart a movement than to have two themes that are in your face and represent a message that resonates. Chosen, was the first word that came to mind, when thinking how I could identify with myself and let others know, that I was Meant to Be.

If you're Chosen, then you have been designated to possess certain expectations that you must meet, and this potential was written precisely for you and you alone. Now we all have to figure out, what we are Chosen to do or become.

Picking who you are designated to become may seem like a daunting task, but in time it is revealed to you with clarity and helps you to have confidence and courage.

To Seek

Why must we seek? *"They say all that wander are not lost."* (J. R. R. Tolkien) With that thought in mind, do you want to wander all the time? Do you not want to move or seek with determination or for a specific resolution?

> *You will seek Me and find Me*
> *when you seek Me with all your heart.*
> -Jeremiah 29:13

If you're chosen to seek, then you must pursue with all your heart. You must pledge yourself unconditionally and without any hesitancy.

To Serve

A servant leader is what I ambitiously sought to emulate and convey to others as I went through many years as a senior advisor in the US Army. Why? That was based directly on my developmental process that was derived from a helpful foundation. I was fortunate to have amazing mentors and senior guides when I first joined the Army. There was a collective of over 100 years' time in service that I was directly assigned to and mentored by at Fort Bragg, North Carolina. These great teachers set me on a path and that would ensure my trajectory and potential for advancement was limitless.

How many people can say they're chosen to serve? I would venture to say more people would say they were chosen to lead versus serve. Everyone wants to be in charge, and everyone wants to make decisions, but not everyone wants to put in the work to be given the chance.

The best way to realize the right thing to do is to understand that easy isn't challenging. Not much thought required. The right thing is easy to recognize as it usually is the hardest thing to do.

To Succeed

Chosen to succeed, this is what we all hope for without fail. We all hope and pray for triumph. I don't think most people realize or want to admit, achievement is the product of hard work. You're not guaranteed that through your efforts that success will be automatic.

The equation for success, is outlined in a fluid formula that states when hard work and preparation meet opportunity thrives. If you are equipped when your opportunities arise, then you will succeed. Could it be that easy? I would answer this in two ways, yes it can be that easy if you utilize what you have prepared for deliberately. The contrast or the alternative is that you do not use your skills or any previous preparation that you may have when your opportunity arises. Both require choice and those selections are relative to you as a person.

Success is relative to the person who is evaluating the victory or success of an assignment. But, if you were chosen, should you have to work as hard? I would argue that we are all chosen and that we all should win through our life with the certainty that hard work and thoughtful conduct is rewarded.

The passionate pursuit of Purpose should directly influence your action and thereby your achievements. This should be evident in anything and everything you do.

COMMITTED ◆

And may your hearts be fully committed to the LORD our God, to live by His decrees and obey His commands, as at this time.
-1 Kings 8:61

*Commit to the LORD whatever you do,
and He will establish your plans.*
-Proverbs 16:3

TO STRUGGLE

Commitment to go through stress, struggle, and hardships are not things people are going out of their way to be involved with or freely take on. We all have problems and although we don't think of it that way, we are fundamentally committed to the course laid out before us. This informs our behavior and what it teaches is immeasurable to our character development. Character is courage combined with conviction.

I would say that to be a character is completely different than having character. Personality can intrude and is something that can foster development or hinder personal progress and self-awareness through struggle.

Our commitment to struggle is not a connection that we enter blindly. The fact is that we must stand up in the face of adversity. We must take the challenge on directly and with conviction. When we do, we are ready to move to the next step which would be to fight.

To Fight

Who commits to fight? And why?

The truth of the matter is that we are all fighters. We are all aggressive at different levels. We have a choice on how much aggression we want to be involved in.

When you tie the first two phrases together, to struggle and to fight, this leads me back to something that I've discussed previously: action. You need action and commitment in anything you do. Because as mentioned in (James 2:17), *"Faith without works, is dead."* It also ties with the fact that we should find joy in the struggle because it allows our perseverance to develop and expose others to the benefits that remaining committed and focused can provide.

To Overcome

God doesn't call the qualified, He qualifies the called. If you're to overcome, do you need to be an expert, not at all. Is there a certain skill or attribute that you will need? The answer is that what we need comes to us mysteriously and at the exact right moment. A rather baffling blessing.

You ever wonder why God chooses the instruments that He does to serve His requests. Chosen and Committed are two key values that denote the phases of mentorship within a nonprofit organization, Bigger Than Sports, South Carolina that I'm fortunate to be a board member of, which was started by a great young man of faith and resolve, Jay Spearman. Jay's story is a phenomenal testament to perseverance that led to a passionate pursuit of his Purpose.

A sense of duty and or a burden to lead produces joy and provides confirmation of your journey. I've been blessed to have met him and I appreciate his friendship, his counsel, and his desire to give back to his community through personal constructive involvement.

Simplifying things for me helped me comprehend them and remain fixed in my memory. I suggest to you an unassuming task, as a believer, use your own ABC platform to write out your own list of convictions.

CHAPTER 4

THE ABC'S OF BELIEVING – ALL BELIEVER'S CHOOSE (ABC)

MY "26" CONVICTIONS OF CHOICE THROUGH VERSES ♦

Atonement: Amends in Christ
He shall burn all the fat on the altar as he burned the fat of the fellowship offering. In this way the priest will make atonement for the leader's sin, and he will be forgiven. -Leviticus 4:26

Benevolence: Generosity in Christ
Because of the service by which you have proved yourselves, others will praise God for the obedience that accompanies your confession of the gospel of Christ, and for your generosity in sharing with them and with everyone else. -Corinthians 9:13

Confidence: Assurance in Christ
The fruit of that righteousness will be peace; its effect will be quietness and confidence forever. -Isaiah 32:17

Devotion: Spiritual Fullness in Christ
So then, just as you received Christ Jesus as Lord, continue to live your lives in Him, rooted and built up in Him, strengthened in the faith as you were taught, and overflowing with thankfulness. See to it that no one takes you captive through hollow and deceptive philosophy, which depends on human tradition and the elemental spiritual forces of this world rather than on Christ.
-Colossians 2: 6-8

Empathy: Compassion in Christ
Be kind to one another, tenderhearted, forgiving one another, as God in Christ forgave you. -Ephesians 4:32

Faith: Trust in Christ
Now faith is the assurance of things hoped for, the conviction of things not seen. -Hebrews 11:1

Grace: Elegance in Christ
For through the law I died to the law, so that I might live to God. I have been crucified with Christ. It is no longer I who live, but Christ who lives in me. And the life I now live in the flesh I live by faith in the Son of God, who loved me and gave Himself for me. I do not nullify the grace of God, for if righteousness were through the law, then Christ died for no purpose. -Galatians 2: 19-21

Humility: Modesty in Christ
For everyone who exalts himself will be humbled, and he who humbles himself will be exalted. -Luke 14:11

Integrity: Truth in Christ
The integrity of the upright guides them, but the crookedness of the treacherous destroys them. -Proverbs 11:3

Joy: Delight in Christ
You make known to me the path of life; in Your presence there is fullness of joy; at Your right hand are pleasures forevermore. -Psalms 16:11

Knowledge: Familiarity in Christ
The fear of the Lord is the beginning of knowledge; fools despise wisdom and instruction. -Proverbs 1:7

Love: Kindness in Christ
A new commandment I give to you, that you love one another: just as I have loved you, you also are to love one another. By this all people will know that you are My disciples, if you have love for one another. -John 13: 34-35

Mercy: Forgiveness in Christ
For judgment is without mercy to one who has shown no mercy. Mercy triumphs over judgment. -James 2:13

Needs: Desires in Christ
And my God will supply every need of yours according to His riches in glory in Christ Jesus. -Philippians 4:19

Obedience: Compliance in Christ
Jesus answered him, "If anyone loves Me, he will keep My word, and My Father will love him, and We will come to him and make Our home with him." -John 14:23

Passion: Longing in Christ
My soul longs, yes, faints for the courts of the Lord; my heart and flesh sing for joy to the living God. -Psalms 84:2

Quest: Mission in Christ
The thief comes only to steal and kill and destroy. I came that they may have life and have it abundantly. -John 10:10

Righteousness: Virtue in Christ
For Christ is the end of the law for righteousness to everyone who believes. -Romans 10:4

Serve: Oblige in Christ
For even the Son of Man came not to be served but to serve, and to give His life as a ransom for many. -Mark 10:45

Talent: Gift in Christ
As each has received a gift, use it to serve one another, as good stewards of God's varied grace. -1 Peter 4:10

Understanding: Be Considerate in Christ
The purpose in a man's heart is like deep water, but a man of understanding will draw it out. -Proverbs 20:5

Values: Have Ideals in Christ
For what will it profit a man if he gains the whole world and forfeits his soul? Or what shall a man give in return for his soul?
-Matthew 16:26

Wisdom: Insight in Christ
The beginning of wisdom is this: Get wisdom, and whatever you get, get insight. -Proverbs 4:7

X-perience: Involvement in Christ
But the one who did not know, and did what deserved a beating, will receive a light beating. Everyone to whom much was given, of him much will be required, and from him to whom they entrusted much, they will demand the more. -Luke 12:48

Youth: Innocence in Christ
May our sons in their youth be like plants full grown, our daughters like corner pillars cut for the structure of a palace. -Psalms 144:12

Zeal: Enthusiasm in Christ
For out of Jerusalem shall go a remnant, and out of Mount Zion a band of survivors. The zeal of the Lord of hosts will do this.
-Isaiah 37:32

This compilation or summary suggests that we all should observe and work towards the virtuous path. This collection of verses is not all inclusive, this is what I chose to affirm for myself. Keep things simple, the ABC approach works for me, and it might work for you as well. I challenge you to read this verse and put it into practice in your life; *For unto whomsoever much is given, of him shall be much required.* (Luke 12:48)

LEADERSHIP PRINCIPLES

I think as we move forward and expand on the various areas of the IM2B Movement, it is imperative to discuss how to be a leader first. We all are charged with possessing and conveying the qualities of leadership. I would submit that we are all expected to be a Servant Leader. If we take the example of Jesus Christ as our way to walk, find and survey our resolve, then how could we avoid following such an exemplary example.

Jesus Christ provides us all with an appropriate example of, "How to Be." Servant is a word that has many connotations, I would infer most are negative. So, think of service as better to be helpful, forgiving, and willing to make a difference and then perhaps you can give of yourself in a meaningful and thoughtful way.

The greatest leader to walk the earth said in (Matthew 4:19), *"Follow Me, and I will make you fishers of men."* There are so many "self-help books" or "how to guides" when it comes to leadership, yet they all seem to pale in comparison to this simple statement. Follow Me. If you follow Me, I will teach you how to have others yearn to follow you. A remarkable, yet simple way to interpret the world.

Ideologies rooted in Biblical themes tend to enliven both the heart and mind. Why? Because we need to believe in something larger than ourselves. As Blaise Pascal said, *"What is the disadvantage of believing in a Higher Source, God. NONE."*

Quite the opposite. If you ignore the existence of a higher life source, then you yourself may feel justified in living a life where you squander the opportunity to see what is truly beautiful and glorious about the world. Cynicism teaches nothing, but indifference to suffering and rationalizing contempt for others who need help.

Think about who Jesus chose to be His disciples. Were they their time's Fortune 500 CEO's or typical influential religious leaders? Absolutely not! God does not call on the qualified, He qualifies the called fits directly into how He searched out the men He chose. Let that sink in when you read it, if it doesn't, then read it again. He was calculated in His search to select men who had the potential and just required this proposition, to follow a person who they recognized as being the Truth and the Light.

I believe Jesus was speaking not only to the Disciples when He made that offer to them, but He was also talking to the Pharisees. He demonstrated pure qualities He sought by His act of selection, and in turn He now was telling everyone else, watch what I'm going to do, with them. These men would embark on a journey down a pathway that they never knew was predetermined for them, to spread His Word.

> *When He had finished washing their feet,*
> *He put on His clothes and returned to His place. "Do you understand what I have done for you?" He asked them. "You call me 'Teacher' and 'Lord,' and rightly so, for that is what I am. Now that I, your Lord and Teacher, have washed your feet, you also should wash one another's feet. I have set you an example that you should do as I have done for you. Very truly I tell you, no servant is greater than his master, nor is a messenger greater than the one who sent him. Now that you know these things, you will be blessed if you do them."*
> -John 13:12-17

Jesus gave unto His disciples the gift of service through reciprocation. He invested in them continuously throughout His time and encouraged them to share this benefit with others. We can get so caught up in the what we can't, won't or even don't do. I would suggest that we forget what we "have to" do, which is live with Purpose.

As an experienced manager and supervisor, I came to an early understanding that I needed a guideline, or some set of ideologies to keep me morally tethered.

The following is my vision of what I used as a style template and what I shared with my future junior and senior leaders that I had the honor of serving with.

CHAPTER 6

THE ABC'S OF LEADERSHIP: FIVE PRINCIPLES

(write down your ABC's of leadership, these are the ones I used)
Accountability, Balance, Commitment, Development, Engagement.

The truth is that this is far from an end all be all list. I used the ABC's to guide me in a simple and easily applicable way to manage and encourage others.

When you think about **accountability** what comes to mind? I would directly associate accountability and responsibility. I am certain you should be accountable for your actions and in turn, not by your fault, but by default, this will act as an example for others to do the right thing. I must be liable for my activities and my words and not allow myself to excuse anything regardless as to how my communications were conveyed and how they could also be misconstrued.

Balance is extremely key to your overall success. The sooner you learn a sense of stability in your personal and professional life, the more fruitful you will be in your own respective job. Stability is not confined to just our personal and professional lives, it should be appreciated in all aspects of living. Take time to appreciate instances in your life at the moment they occur.

Force yourself to take a walk, sit down, or spend time device free. Though it is easy to explore the need to connect, it is habitual and not that helpful in being able to see another in their fullness. It is easy to become preoccupied with distractions such as electronic devices whose sole purpose is to distract, and yet people somehow feel connected though they are all alone together. So, our quest to be social conflicts with our need for discovery and insight, we are drawn further away from social interaction.

I know, it sounds crazy, but just do it, go device free for a period. We need time to sit down and reflect on where we have been, where we are, and where we are going. We need to take into account and appreciate the what and why we're here.

Commitment goes without saying. If you're not committed to the task at hand, then what is the point in completing it. You must be certain that this is what you need to do or what you need to be involved with. Obligation is something we have to choose unconditionally. We need to accept this responsibility and complete the goal it requires without any hesitation or reservations.

Development starts from within. You need to learn that through progress, you will develop yourself. You as a leader need to mature and challenge yourself. You need to encourage your subordinates to continue to cultivate their skillset towards development. So, when there is development in all directions amongst a group, then there is a direct correlation and even a cyclical approach to the group's overall success. Change yourself and in turn you help others around you. It goes back to the aspire to inspire others, through your conduct.

Having **engagement** with the others you lead is vital to your achievement of the goals you have as a team. You can take a moment and get to know those who support you, what makes them tick, what issues they have. Would you not agree that this would give you insight on the pulse of that person?

There is a direct association between knowing who someone is and what makes them operate, their productivity level or output. In the Army there were a lot of regulations and guidelines that I followed, but there was one standard that stuck with me and it was in the counseling manual. The, "follow up," was a must and required when we complete or receive counseling.

Think about this, we are required to follow up after we counsel or give instructions. We know that we have given the order or a message, we can confirm acknowledgement and receipt, but the question is: how do we know that we were right in our counsel? The follow up ties this all together because now you can lay out what you've discussed, what were your goals, and see if there was a true understanding or if it fell short of what your expectations of what you thought needed to be completed.

We will now look at some of the traits that I considered to be important. These five values are not inclusive or exclusive to what will define a successful leader, these are but few that I used consistently during my career.

Chapter 7

Professional Attributes

Once again, I used the same thought process when I think about what attributes or characteristics you should have to be successful.

The ABC's of Professional Attributes ◆
(write down your strengths that you have and that you may need to be effective)

Attitude, Beliefs, Character, Discipline, Empathy

First and foremost, your **attitude** is crucial to any accomplishment you might have in a professional setting. A controlled temperament is indicative of maturity and will be a positive contribution in your interactions and connections.

You must have a set of norms or a **belief** system that you are vested in. If you do, it will be evident in how fruitful your interactions are with another. Rooted in trust you will exude confidence and exude competence.

Your **character** must be beyond reproach. It should reverberate in anything you undertake. You must be an upstanding person with respectful bearing and willingness to listen and do the right thing no matter the cost.

Jesus' followers were called "Disciples" let that sink in. A disciple more commonly is known as a follower of a teacher. Do you need **discipline** to follow? I would say without a doubt: a resounding YES!

This is paramount to your accomplishment. Self-control and discipline are an expectation that all leaders should emulate.

To me, this is one of the most underestimated attributes we need to discuss. There is a huge difference between sympathy and **empathy**. The emotional attachment or connection you will have as an empathetic leader is required to keep you engaged with your team. This is an essential quality in any leader.

Empathy is often viewed as a weakness, but it is an honest connection with someone to let them know that you may not have been through the same thing. This trait can illustrate that you are willing to share their pain in going through a trial. As a leader, I took pride in considering all aspects and involvements when making decisions that impacted young men and women's lives directly. To see myself in another made me aware of the value of empathy.

When you combine the leadership principles with the professional attributes, there is evidence that our influences lead to differences for all of us individually. Specifically, I would offer that we cause our own conflicts or internal strife through limits.

Through these restrictions we must figure out what confines us. What factors influence us and why? I want to introduce my point of view on the difference in the limitations we may face throughout our lives.

Limitations (Self-Imposed Limitations versus External Limitations)

Self-Imposed Limitations ♦

The top five reasons we limit ourselves are listed below for discussion.

I. We focus on failure.
II. We choose to follow another person's path, more than we choose our own path.
III. We don't accept our Purpose and live that Purpose consistently.
IV. We give up too easily.
V. We lack faith and hope.

Faith by itself isn't enough. Unless it produces good deeds, it is dead and useless. Faith must compel a person to navigate the world in a thoughtful and morally responsible way.
-James 2:17

Why do we focus on failure so much? We live in an instant satisfaction and self-indulgent driven society. If we don't receive instantaneous gratification, then we equate that to failure. Impatience is the root cause of a lack of willingness to appreciate the long and arduous trail of our Purpose.

Is it easier to choose someone else's track or follow someone else on their journey or their quest for self-actualization? The question is does it work? The answer remains unresolved, absolutely. We gravitate to others exploits and why not given that we associate that directly with the appearance of success. We like, or we follow, or we stop what we are doing to concern ourselves with others. This leads us back to my original premise of, are you passionately chasing your own Purpose.

When you don't accept that notion as valid or as incomprehensible, then where are you heading with your life. What is your guiding light or what value do you have, if your determination is not at the forefront? Are you thoughtlessly driven by your instinctive actions and behavior? Only you could respond to that question and I encourage you to take time to, "have a think on it."

We quit. We just give up because that is the easy way out. Robert Fritz, author of The Path of Least Resistance says, *"If you limit your choice only to what seems possible or reasonable, you disconnect yourself from what you truly want, and all that is left is a compromise."*

> *"Most people never get there. They're afraid or unwilling to demand enough of themselves and take the easy road, the path of least resistance...If you're not pushing yourself beyond the comfort zone, if you're not constantly demanding more from yourself–expanding and learning as you go–your choosing a numb existence. Your denying yourself an extraordinary trip."*
> -Dean Karnazes

We don't want to challenge ourselves with anything that might help us grow and advance to a higher level. Why? Is this a learned response? Fear often is the result of timidity or better, insecurity. It obscures our vision and makes the possible seem improbable and therefore can cause paralysis and self-doubt.

I would encourage you to sit down and begin to write down, what it is that stops you from doing what you're meant to do.

When you get this written out, put it to the side for now because I will ask you another question soon and I would like you to compare that question to the answers of this question. My hopes are they will produce some great thoughts and provide some insight into the person you are. I will ask you one question that you will need to mull over and that you'll have to come back to. Does your Purpose override any of the reasons you've decided to stop what you're supposed to do? If no, then I must ask you, why not? I would challenge you to think this through and encourage to accept your Purpose and begin to live on and with it.

Lastly, we lack faith and hope. As I've stated previously, these two deeds require an action. Basically put, we need to act, to make sure that faith and hope doesn't permit despair to rule our lives.

And without faith it is impossible to please Him, for whoever would draw near to God must believe that He exists and that He rewards those who seek Him.
-Hebrews 11:6

Can we tolerate not having faith? Better yet, should we tolerate or endure such a notion. The Word informs us, that He rewards those who seek Him, seek Him faithfully.

Through Him we have also obtained access by faith into this grace in which we stand, and we rejoice in hope of the glory of God. More than that, we rejoice in our sufferings, knowing that suffering produces endurance, and endurance produces character, and character produces hope, and hope does not put us to shame, because God's love has been poured into our hearts through the Holy Spirit who has been given to us.
-Romans 5:2-5

There is no shame in hope this passage decrees. And love is the eternal source of life ingrained into our spirit that transcends any lack of hope or faith. Think about why and how you limit yourself and jot that down. Keep that list handy as we move into the next self-set of restrictions.

External Limitations ◆

External or outside factors can impact our limits as well. Here are my top five:

I. Social
II. Technological
III. Political
IV. Legal
V. Economical

SOCIAL

When we think of a limitation, would you initially consider that you are socially limited? I would say that would not be your first choice, but it would be a selection that you would pick eventually. I placed social first because I think we are taught that being social is an attribute worth mastering from an early age as human survival demands it. This is nonnegotiable.

We learn right from wrong and a host of other things that show contrast. Though to be clear we can be either helped or hindered by these initial social limitations. These define who we are, how we look at things, and why we react the way we do.

When things seem or are described as socially unacceptable, does that not influence everyone in that society. We are social creatures, we enjoy intermingling with one another, in some capacity. Whether it be a small or large group setting, or just on an individual basis. The issue is as social beings we gravitate towards being social often. We are drawn in, like a moth to a flame.

Technological

I struggled with not putting this one number one on my list, but I had to have a foundation of social interactions. A close second in my opinion is our technology and how it confines us today. We are in a society that social media has exponentially increased our need to relate and its relevance has manifested in the past 20 to 30 years, more than any other period we have been through.

Think about all the technological advances we have made, just in the past 50 years. It is phenomenal to see all that has been developed and shared. It is amazing that there are people out there ardently trying to justify their existence and then in contrast there are others that remain consumed with technology. God gives each one of us a unique and special talent. When we realize we have that ability we must pass it on and share it with others.

Words are a tool we must use to communicate yet they are often misconstrued. The question is why, and while context is often distorted or worse completely associated with meaning that was unintended. Technology specifically has reduced our drive and our willingness to use critical thinking combined with our analog based skills that we possess. The point of which is to facilitate understanding rather than its opposite, confusion.

Political

Well, this is a slippery slope, to instigate or to evaluate. What I will say is that we choose sides and based on our choice we sometimes can walk blindly towards and follow what that association may say or do. It is great to connect or lean towards a certain group or opinion; but should we put that affiliation before our own free will or thought?

I accept as true that we directly affect others and indirectly influence more with our choices then we often take credit for. This holds true in the political realm. This is an area that divides the purest and simplest of relationships and bonds. The reason is that we tend to think and believe in absolutes, but we forget that these political sides are all man made and we should be very cautious on how much we can trust and rely on what they embody.

LEGAL

There are some things that others can do, that some groups cannot do. Is this a true statement? I think that the statement is true based on my life experiences. There are numerous instances that can support this statement. There are polarizing stories in various media outlets that amplify this statement. From a legal standpoint, what limitations can come in to play when we start to think about our Purpose. When you assert your intentions, could you be infringing on someone else's passions or their way of life?

To me, the legal aspect of limitations is a discussion that maybe should be left to another to explain. Because the legal and political platforms, especially today, are viewed by everyone so differently. There is an us vs them mentality and that causes dissension and allows for an inaccurate control of dialogue, where mere assertions pass for facts. This way of thinking would be a naïve intellectually lazy way to understand the world.

Disparagement, skepticism and anger cloud our judgement and influence our conversations. This way of thinking isn't useful in a democracy. The consequences of which are the preventions of constructive public civil discourse that undermines our collective sense of common interests and is a basis of today's polarization.

ECONOMICAL

How often do we make an excuse about what we can or cannot do based merely on our economical standing? Should we base our commitment solely on a financial influence. I think we tend to focus too much on that specifically and it leads to preventing us from helping others.

Think about the following statement and how many times you've used it or how many times you've heard someone else use it. I don't have the money right now to help, but I would love to help when possible moving forward.

This goes back to the idea of self-imposed limitations. We are all very well intended, but are inclined to rationalize our reluctance to be helpful. You can say I want to, but I can't.

Let that sink in. How can we be well intentioned, but then in the same moment, impose limits and not be intentional with them. This is truly the dilemma we find ourselves in and the truth is, once again, action is missing. Intention is defined by action.

Accomplishment can be described or characterized as your, "why." Through this achievement we can define our successes and in turn recognize why we do things. So, here we are again, back to our premise of what should we do and how do we actively engage in this path consistently.

Questions should provoke and promote thought and through that insight answers should then result. Let's take a journey into all the basic inquiries that come to mind with regard to our foundational idea that we are here for a specific reason and we possess meaning.

Who Puts Us On Our Path To Purpose?

The short answer to this question – God.

> *But I have raised you up for this very Purpose,
> that I may show you My power and that My name might be
> proclaimed in all the earth.*
> -Exodus 9:16

The extended version is that there are many people, situations, environmental considerations, and a host of other factors that can claim to be a part of your drive and your route. Let's tackle this one in segments that we can easily review.

People ◆

"A mirror reflects a man's face, but what he is really like is shown by the kind of friends he chooses."
-Colin Powell

The people you choose or that you allow into your life reflect or offer awareness to the person you are and the things you accept. The question I have or that I pose is, how do you control what people or which people you surround yourself with?

Do you control who you are born to? Where you are born? When you are born? We can all agree, the answer is no. However, let us take a further look into this from a different perspective and shed some light and answer some questions that you may have about yourself and your life.

The first people in your life are traditionally your parents or in some cases your extended family. In other cases, loving families who open their homes to children who have no family. This does not cover every possibility, but this gives us a baseline to operate from.

Ideally our parents are charged with our care, our education, and preparing us to integrate into society as a productive member. How? Is there a specific book that will cover all these things?

There are a host of how to books and articles that are written to assist new parents on their voyage and give them the principles and guidelines to successfully raise a young adult. The problem is, that we all have a different mold and we generally won't fit into anyone else's ideal. How do you help these parents recognize when all children have a different potential or a different pathway?

The "people" are what drive us down this thoroughfare, and they are the ones who will forever influence our thoughts and our considerations of what it is we are meant to do or better yet, what it is we are "Meant To Be".

> *Teach children how they should live,*
> *and they will remember it all their life.*
> -Proverbs 22:6

I want to give an example to really and effectively illustrate this thought. Children are often seen as the seed or the offspring of their parents – a direct reflection of two people who have joined in a union to create and bring them into this world. Children are planted seeds in their parents' lives. They must be given love, be nurtured and cared for, they must be educated and provided for, and they will take these traits and grow. So, if you plant a seed, what are some of the things that are required to assist that seed in its growth to flower and blossom.

First, you must start with good soil to plant the seeds. I think that parents and the children's immediate family are the soil. I think, children must have a solid foundation or a solid base to be planted into and they will grow. It is imperative that the preliminary phase in your life, your formative years, are filled with people who are living their life the right way – whose goal should be to pour into you (the child). Now, we can get down into the weeds and lose focus on the fact that we all are born in different societies and cultures or countries. The reality is, things are all relative to your own situation.

Focus on the task at hand, addressing the people that have been put in your life to set you off on your expedition that has been written specifically for you. Other people are very important, and they are the key to you and your growth, they will either be a direct influence on your progress and will serve as guides for your success. If not, then you will embark on a lifelong pursuit of self-discovery in solitude. A quest of sorts loaded with hazards and no reliable guide.

Second, you must not be restricted. When you first plant a seed, you keep it tucked in a small confined space, to watch over and you can nurture it. As the seed takes form and begins to bloom and grow, so does the space that it requires. It now needs to be able to grow, at a pace suited for itself and in an area that promotes change.

Like most things that require growth and to be nurtured, we now come to a pivotal stage of when does coddling and encouraging advancements towards adulthood, become enabling and hindering. This is a razor thin line that is traversed often with trepidation and fear of reprisal or resentment.

Seeds will start to bud and turn into flowers that are planted. These flowers or plants will outgrow their pot. This holds true for children as well. You are born into a loving and caring environment where things are provided for you, but you will inevitably have to learn to fend for yourself.

You ever notice a tree, if planted in good soil, and nurtured, will grow beautifully in optimal conditions. There are no impediments. The tree grows both above ground and expands its roots below ground. The tree has been embedded in good soil and cultivated. Now, the tree grows towards the sun, its new source of life, fulfilling its Purpose to live and provide a resource that is necessary for survival.

The same could be said about children. Parents and other individuals in the children's lives must learn to step back and allow the child to obtain life experiences that produce learning without any interference.

Environment ◆

Next, we tackle the environmental considerations that directly influence or affect children. We have all heard the saying a, "product of my environment", but what does that mean and who would assert such a thing, without allowing for an excuse to explain self-responsibility.

If we are talking environments, then we are now presenting a stimulus, or some sort of external factor not specifically associated with you. This unknown, the environment, plays a role in the who you are, what your exposure is to certain things, where you are from, when and how you are exposed to life, and why you think or react the way you do.

We can go through a variety of examples, but to keep it in categories we will speak to the following situations. The first is a loving and caring family setting, where all members of the family are actively involved in the child's life. Secondly, we will discuss where a segment of the family that is not involved and has no interaction or assistance in that child's progress. The last condition would be the child grows up absent of a family, where they are forced to take on independent learning. A kind of self-taught way of learning, mostly through trial and error.

The first category would be the more traditional view of family and early childhood development. That is to say, that given a foundation of parents, loving and caring relations, access to education and the correct societal stimulus, this child may possess a predetermined advantage towards success. As we know, this is far from the case. Perspective on what and who are involved in the early stages of a child's growth can change from society to society, culture to culture, socioeconomic standings and many more factors.

So, specifically in this first group, what would be the things that encourage the child to embrace the privilege simply to live? I would say that their "why" is a mystery to them, but is somehow innate and thus lives within. The stimulus and the opportunity afforded in this first grouping would be more favorable for an antiquated definition of success, but as we all know there is no guarantee of success in the business and coping in life.

The second category would be for intermittent or sparse family involvement or contribution in the child's life. This child would not have access or availability to some of the family members that the first group would have. How would this affect or limit that child? In most cases, you can argue that it is not a restriction, but potentially an enrichment. Struggle breeds success. If we wipe away all the money, neighborhoods, and other advantages and just leave the people, then is being a product of your environment truly an end all be all determining factor? A resounding no!

We now look at the third class, a child who has inadequate to no interaction with family. A child who is brought up in a system or by a nontraditional means. What does this look like? Are these children one step behind their contemporaries on their road to triumph? The fact is that coveting and expecting normalcy and missing its absence can serve as a great motivator.

If we lined all three categories of kids up, shoulder to shoulder, would you be able to put them in their aforementioned group at different stages in their lives? I think that it is easier on us, to try and pigeonhole and place people into some sort of box. So, we would like to think that we could easily pick these children out, but the reality is, it would all depend on the child themselves not us. Choice is what God provides us all with, the privileged as well as the deprived.

How many kids know, learn and embrace their God given gifts, and at what age do they do so? If you have opportunity does that equate to victory? One could argue that triumph is comparable to your own sense of who you are, once again debunking any specific categorizing of these groups. There are kids that just will exceed expectations defying what others thought them capable of.

What if we changed our viewpoint, what if we thought of other possibilities into the mix? Are we a product of our environment or more directly are we a product of our decisions? This comes back to the simple and most basic right, we all have. The right of "choice" is a learned behavior no matter where you grow up or what group you reside in.

Our choices are somewhat predisposed by our environment or our exposure for sure. But to simply state, I'm a product of my environment, is to accept that you are giving up one of your most basic rights and one of the first things you have as a learned behavior, acceptance of the inevitable rather than choice.

You ever just sit back and just marvel at what accomplishments we have had the fortunate privilege to witness in our life? I often sit and reflect and think how someone ever thought to create this or that, and the truth is, God blesses everyone to make a difference and we are fortunate that there have been some great people who have accepted and pursued their goals.

We all come from different walks of life and diverse backgrounds, but we sometimes overlook or undervalue those differences. All like items can be or seem boring, a rainbow is a collection of colors that stops us all in our tracks to appreciate. Can we not just simplify life in that manner? That we are here for a greater good, to join one side to another, one part of an amazing color spectrum. You ever wonder why after it rains that a rainbow appears? Is it a sign of hope?

Does this rainbow only appear in certain regions or neighborhoods or to certain people? This is a gift that we should all take time to appreciate and to embrace. Things of beauty exist all around us and yet we walk by being stuck in a mindset, I'm a product of my environment.

What Is The Pursuit of Purpose With Passion?

Passion is defined as an intense desire or enthusiasm for something. So, how many people are eager to pursue their role with that desire? What drives us?

What is your Purpose? Write it down, put it to the side and continue to read, and as you read, put some thought to, am I avidly in pursuit of it. We are driven by things that are common to us or subjects that are known and thoughts that are understood. Take your other notes out on Purpose now and begin to compare them.

We are all raised in a **different** manner, but we often meet on our journey and share some commonalities with others on our voyages.

It would be presumptive to say that it is far less common to see individuals in an obsessive **pursuit** of what describes them today. Why? If we all have a reason to live and a goal, then what should guide and direct our thoughts and activities? Why do we not fervently pursue what is expected of us?

The short answer is discovery, and many of us can't accept that we wander around lost and confused. The truth is, we are living in a day and age where we are growing daily in all aspects of society. Our technological growth rate is tremendous, and our norms continue to alter and adapt to what is now **socially** accepted. The essence of this is that we, as a society have willingly made a choice and that choice is to do anything and everything that suits us personally or now.

We live in a time that we want instant gratification and, in a time where technology supports, in **fact** encourages, this enjoyment. So, do we lack an appetite or a hankering for knowledge, or do we lack focus?

I would say focus is absent overall today. Your attention is diverted from your potential. People have no issue focusing on reality television or their social media feeds, but are these distractions to you and restrict your thoughts and activities? Yes, and unfortunately it is only going to get worse before it gets any better.

> *"Where ignorance is bliss, 'tis folly to be wise."*
> *-Thomas Gray's poem,*
> *"Ode on a Distant Prospect of Eton College," 1742*

Generational gaps exist more and more today because of the evolution in technology. This progress has caused people to lose focus on themselves and **underscore** the provocation of knowing in a moment, what is going on across the entire world. This yearning or this overwhelming necessity for information has been misused by some and ignored by others who should be concerned.

Do we indulge in our cravings for knowledge as much as we follow our social media **feeds** or as much as we require instant gratification? Absolutely not, we are in a time now that more than ever people need Purpose. The divisiveness and the hate are amplified by our social media growth.

So, reflecting on the Thomas Gray quote about ignorance being blissful, we are now living in a time where with infinite access to information from every corner and area of this world are now simply just a click away. The ease and access to knowing, reading or hearing about something that directly influences you and your thoughts and feeds your biases, is completely obtainable to you. This distraction and this availability of access to data justify and ignores our desires to be real. Moreover, it provides us with a legitimate excuse to focus on what is truly meaningful in life.

Are we in a time that people will lose their focus and themselves? Who is fighting to keep "you" at the **forefront**? Is it the Church, religious leaders or political figures? I would suggest that we are fighting within ourselves regularly. Fighting recurrent distractions to seek God and serve others.

Think about what motivates you day-to-day. What is significant to one is not necessarily vital to the next? However, all of us are directly associated. We are all **here**, now, specifically and have a greater Purpose. It is greater than one person, it is greater than the group.

The task is to see this, recognize this and then accept it. When you do all three, the final step would be to choose to share your talents. How often do we take an easy wrong over the hard right? Our decisions have second and third order effects that impede our route. Although I believe we will continue on a predetermined course. There will be other obstacles or barriers we must overcome and suffer based on our choices, as life instructs, even those who refuse to learn.

It is understandable to not want to take a chance not want to expose ourselves to any possibility of being vulnerable because we know and remember what failure looks like and how it feels.

Consider it pure joy, my brothers and sisters, whenever you face trials of many kinds, because you know that the testing of your faith produces perseverance. Let perseverance finish its work so that you may be mature and complete, not lacking anything.
-James 1:2-4

This verse resonates to me as it drives me, it has made me realize so much and helped me to accept things in my life because it isn't a contest or an endurance test. The test is, to smile, smile in the face of adversity. We are designed to learn through adversity or through struggle. If things were easy or there was no resistance, would we take control of our own lives? Life intrudes and its purpose from beginning to end is withheld from us, yet we must prevail, and struggle as less and less can make sense.

I share this verse with so many, and it is appropriate for all our struggles. We all go through pain, loss, struggle, doubt, and despair. Issues are universal in and on our path that defines us as humans. So, why should we all not share and adhere to this verse?

Let's take it frame by frame. Consider it pure joy when you face trials, who in their right mind would want to say that? Yes, please give me more adversity, thank you very much, this is exactly what I was looking for today. But seriously, it **is** a true statement, when it is coupled with the rest. The joy comes from the fact that you know your faith is being tested and you're learning how to persevere, you're learning how to adapt and overcome. Suffering is the quintessential instructor in life.

I vividly recall a seven-day period that completely altered the course of my life. Spring of 2000, my wife was in her final trimester of pregnancy and I was **scheduled** to deploy to Bosnia in a humanitarian support role. I was informed on Monday by my Commander that I would be allowed to stay behind while the rest of my team would go forward that Wednesday.

Wednesday comes and goes. All I can remember **was** I stood out on the tarmac waving goodbye knowing I would catch up with my team soon. I went home to prepare for the birth of my second child, thankful for the opportunity that had been afforded to me.

On Thursday evening, I received an odd and unexpected phone call from a doctor in Florida, asking me very specific questions and probing me for information to confirm that I was indeed who I said I was. Once his questions which to me had a feel of an inquisition were complete, he **then** proceeded to tell me that my father had another massive stroke and was in his words, "Only alive because of the machines that he was currently connected to." Our only reason for conversing that evening was that I was my father's DNR, (do not resuscitate), signature authority and he was looking to have me sign this document and take my dad off all the life sustaining measures that were helping him endure.

I hung up and sat down. At 23 the enormity of this moment struck me. I had in just a few short days been hurled onto an emotional rollercoaster, one that had my **full** attention at every turn. I looked at my daughter running around the house and being chased closely behind by my brother, who had now been with us since that past Christmas because our dad felt he needed some structure and stability that we could provide. I remembered the last conversation that I had with my dad was to inform him I was deploying again and that I would let him know when I was settled in.

With all the changes that had happened I never had a chance to inform him that I was going to be able to stay back and watch the birth. I then took a **moment** to myself and came back in the dining room as I began to serve dinner. I mustered up a haphazard attempt at explaining the phone call I just received. My family looked up at me for direction, they were looking for guidance on how to act or what to feel. I knew that I needed to be strong not for myself, but for them.

My reaction now would be permanent and would be the basis of how they would reflect on this time. I **remember** being stunned, my face stoic and emotionless, unplugging almost. At that moment I didn't have time to fret or become emotional. The task at hand was to load up my car with my little brother and myself and leave North Carolina for Florida. I remember looking at my nine-month pregnant wife with my daughter who was a rambunctious and curious child and telling them simply, I will see you soon and daddy loves you.

As I left, and the house disappeared in the rearview mirror, I wondered what was I **going** to do now? How ill prepared was I to take this on? I glanced over at my younger brother in the passenger seat and was fortunately saved by his youth. He did not fully comprehend the journey in which we were embarking on, not at all.

The next morning, I pull into Florida after an uneventful drive and braced myself for the next few moments. We walked upstairs into the hospital and met with the medical staff. They had paperwork that I was required to fill out so that we could bring an administrative end to my father's life. That was it, a stroke of the pen, and at 23 I had determined it was time to let my dad go. This decision seemed daunting and should I or could I even question all the information that was presented to me by the doctors.

This was just day five out of seven for me, but this day is etched in my memory. I don't recall the specifics as well as I used to, but what I do remember was that my dad, who was "only alive" because he was on life support, was taken off and an interesting thing happened next. All his vitals went up, he was in a coma, but he seemed very comfortable laying there in this hospital bed, motionless. I remember the pat on my shoulder as the doctor walked by me and said, "It won't be long now," and removed himself from the room.

After an hour, with his vitals remaining stable and just as strong off life support as they were on, this decision became unnerving to me. What had I just done? How could I have decided to stop fighting? Was it a rash decision?

I left the room and was met by members of his Church and the Funeral Director. His wishes were known by these random men who wanted me to sit in a lounge and read through and sign more paperwork. By this time, family members began to show up, and were reflecting on great times they shared over a lifetime with their brother or uncle or brother-in-law.

I recollect that I was direct and short with the Funeral Director. I told him, he knew my dad's wishes and that I would absolutely follow them. I didn't see the need for me to waste this time being confined to another room with paperwork.

I looked for my brother next, he was with family, eating and smiling so I just went up and rubbed the top of his head as I passed through and began to walk alone down the hall. I just needed a second to myself, a minute to understand and realize that my dad was gone based merely on the fact that I had signed all these papers. The moment was short lived as the door to the intensive care unit opened and more family came into the hospital and I turned more into a guide shuttling them back into his room in the isolation unit.

Here we sat, for what seemed like days in the hours ahead and I listened to story after story that everyone had felt compelled to share during that time. Silence often spurs conversation or the need for others to fill the awkward emptiness. But all I could do was stare from the bed to the heart monitor. It took 15 hours for his body to ease into peace and serenity, and then just like that, he was gone. I had been up from the previous night and had driven without any stopping or resting, and I was physically and mentally exhausted at that instant.

I went back to his condo, which was weird to be in, now that he was gone. I called home and **told** my nine-month pregnant wife that I would be returning home since the funeral arrangements weren't until the middle of next week. She refused to listen and told me that I must stay there with my family and be the man that they needed me to be. The unknown in that statement was unnerving but was mine alone to accept in that moment.

In the back of my mind, my stateside clock was ticking loud. It is strange how you start to think **about** things like that, because even in that minute I realized I was not in control of my own time and that I would soon be required to leave. Because to drive down and be in Florida currently started my leave process which meant that once my leave was up that I would have to go forward and meet my team. Day six was a blur, I honestly don't know what happened that day besides being with family members.

Day seven I was on the phone with my wife and she stopped me and said so calmly, "Hey, let me call you back," to which I responded, "Why?" She said, "my **water** just broke and I need to get to the hospital." As I hung up, I began to think, how did all of this happen in one week. I wasn't even beginning to mourn the loss of my father and my wife was heading to the hospital to have my son as I was hundreds of miles away.

I was only in the United States this week because of my impending child's birth. But I found myself missing out on that moment for another moment, a tragedy had superseded a blessing. When I returned home five days later, I was now in my last week of vacation days I requested and had an exact date that I was flying out on to meet my team. Our family dynamic changed so drastically in seven days and I was about to be out of the picture for the next six months or so.

That last week was a blur. The only thing I remember was packing and changing my mindset yet again to focus on the task ahead in Bosnia. I wondered how my wife would manage and thought how different this deployment would be from others. The reality of separation was more evident now. Time was not so insignificant anymore and to be honest I was unsure how I would be able to handle things **moving** forward with the knowledge and experiences I just obtained.

I heard a coach say, "Adversity lives with the weak and visits the strong." Let that sink in, adversity visits the strong, which would suggest it is a short-term thing. We all face times of hardship or misfortune, but they are temporary. We must not squander the time we have thinking about the time we have lost, because we in turn will inevitably increase our lost time as we do so.

You can't and must not feel alone during times of tribulation because you're not. This is made so clear in the following poem. Take a second to reflect on times you thought you were all alone in despair. This will serve as a gentle reminder that you will never be alone any of your days, for He is always walking with you, step by step.

FOOTPRINTS

One night I dreamed a dream. As I was walking along the beach with my Lord. Across the dark sky flashed scenes from my life. For each scene, I noticed two sets of footprints in the sand, one belonging to me and one to my Lord.

After the last scene of my life flashed before me, I looked back at the footprints in the sand.

I noticed that at many times along the path of my life, especially at the very lowest and saddest times, there was only one set of footprints.

This really troubled me, so I asked the Lord about it. "Lord, You said once I decided to follow You,

You'd walk with me all the way. But I noticed that during the saddest and most troublesome times of my life, there was only one set of footprints.

I don't understand why, when I needed You the most, You would leave me." He whispered, "My precious child, I love you and will never leave you Never, ever, during your trials and testing. When you saw only one set of footprints, It was then that I carried you."

When Do We Accept Our Purpose?

I think this should be a two-part question. I would say not only when we "accept" our Purpose, but then what? Just because we accept it does not mean we use it or that we gravitate towards it at all.

The quest within itself is a lifelong journey. The search is something that should drive you daily from when you arise to when you rest. This pursuit is what we accept as part of the human condition.

It is not a contest, it is a journey, it is a process, it is something that we must continue to love and learn to love. It is something that helps us grow and requires us to continue to grow, daily.

Everyone has their own Purpose, although those individual Purposes should come together to build with one another and assist one another. This is something that is ordained, and this is something that is written specifically in our fabric of our being.

As iron sharpens iron, so one person sharpens another.
-Proverbs 27:17

I am a firm believer in everything that you do is not condensed into a mere incident and leaves an indelible impression. I believe that every action you take must be evaluated and then understood, and every thought that is generated by you, must be learned by you before you can honestly receive the reason why.

What I'm saying is that, you cannot be appreciated, unless you first appreciate yourself. Using appreciation as my example, we must explore this. How can I truly appreciate someone, if I don't appreciate myself? I must learn what appreciation is, what is meant by it, how to appreciate, and why to appreciate. I must be able to comprehend and rationalize this feeling before I can reciprocate it unto others.

The unpretentious principle or the modest focus in your life should be first and foremost to get yourself together. Learn to accept you for you. Learn to be okay with you. Learn to understand that you have a God given talent and that you cannot accept that gift when you're not focused on your life and your goals. There should be a pecking order that you should concentrate on in your life.

This is the "when" moment. When do I dare to accept that my Purpose should drive me constantly? When do I learn that each day is a blessing and the next is not promised? When do I learn to strive to be a better me and in turn help others to be a better them? When do I proclaim my why?

We don't realize how dependent we are to other people. When we open and share with others, this awakens, encourages, and even emboldens people around us to do the same. This step out in faith is a true testament to your courage.

This was what the first part of the statement described, but the last part, that is where I would like to focus. We have stated and professed something that is important to us, but now we must discuss how do we demonstrate that publicly.

How many of us truly share in public? How many of us assert definitively in public? We can share and encourage others in a comfortable setting, but do we do so in an uncomfortable situation? Our levels of ease determine how open we can be with one another. It takes courage to speak your truth.

If you're surrounded by other like-minded individuals, you're more apt to share knowing there will be no backlash or any negative feedback. We are relational creatures and through your comfort level of being in relation with others, that is where you will find the nerve to speak your truth to another. In the face of challenge speak truth to power, repeat that sentence again and then move on.

You ever notice how people are admired when they know who they are, and they share it out loud with others? Sounds like something you've read about it in any books lately, or at all? It would not be a stretch at all to say that Jesus was a true definition of self-proclamation. Think about how He openly shared His points of views and values without fear of reprisal or repercussion to His actions.

He never concerned Himself with the thoughts of what others would say or how they would react to His religious convictions. He was here to show us the transparency of sharing unconditionally and proclaiming without hesitation. We all have a keen sense of understanding what is right from wrong and what we should or should not do, but we continue to make choices daily that lead us down a variety of paths.

> *Then Jesus came near and said to them, "All authority has been given to Me in heaven and on earth. Go, therefore, and make disciples of all nations, baptizing them in the name of the Father and of the Son and of the Holy Spirit, teaching them to observe everything I have commanded you. And remember, I am with you always, to the end of the age."*
> -Matthew 28:18-20

This was quite a bold proclamation, and, in His time, Jesus was considered a radical and He was viewed as a threat. He brings up quite a few intriguing points in these verses. First and foremost, He proclaims, all authority has been given to Him in both Heaven and earth. This statement alone would confound and bring into question so much to anyone who heard Him say it. The tone certain and easily dismissed as arrogant and youthful hubris.

How could a man be given authority both here and in Heaven? This man, who stands before me asserting this, can this be possible to believe and accept. He then follows it up with a declaration. This declaration was just as bold as His proclamation.

He charged his Disciples to go and to spread His message. His message was to teach everyone what He had taught them. He told them to go out and baptize them in the name of the Father and of the Son and of the Holy Spirit. He required not only discipline, but demanded from the men who followed Him, to be loyal and speak to others with conviction.

This, unbeknownst to them, was their Purpose and this was how the Son of God changed all their trajectories. He empowered them with a message that would now fuel their fire and lead them to share the Word globally. How could you not faithfully take this charge from a man who selflessly gave of Himself? Think about what this message or this proclamation was for them to hear and then to process. Lastly, they must go out amongst strangers and speak the message to all they encounter, in order to comply with His wishes and injunction to share His message with the world.

The mission was to get out His Word. As you begin to think about what a declaration is to you, think about those that you influence. The ones that you know that you effect as well as the ones you have no idea that you impact. These are two diverse categories for sure.

My direct sphere of influence are the people I interact with regularly, but the key is that they know me or know of me for sure. This is essential, because there is some sort of built in credibility and it allows trust to build. There is no need to check or question credentials in some cases, because there is an understanding of who the source is that is both reliable and trustworthy.

The part about this that can get tricky is the concerns from others you know. Their bias can influence how they receive the message. They can either lend credence to what you have said, or they can completely disregard their responses can have a similar effect. What I mean by this is that we value what those in our direct or indirect scope think. Why?

This is a learned behavior, we directly associate like or dislike, especially currently with so much dependency on social media to enlighten and contrary to what we need adversely influence the way we think. You can know a like or a dislike simply by a click or a swipe, it is so impersonal, and the sources are unreliable. We need to be cautious in our proclamations because we should be careful with our feelings. We directly tie emotions to responses, another learned behavior.

This is where the last part of Jesus proclamation ties in to us directly. He reminds us that He is always with us to the end of age. Think about that, you have someone who is with you, forever. This someone believes in you and He believes in what you're doing.

So, should we worry or concern ourselves with what others think? How does this change the way you might look at your own sense of duty and obligation? You should start to think about this specifically and view it in a new light. You now know that Jesus, the Son of God, is with you until the end of time.

He is inspiring you and His only injunction to you is to go out and share His Word and His Works. Do this and complete your Purpose. Sounds simple doesn't it, but why is it so hard to proclaim what we are supposed to do as Soldiers for the Lord. To do good is to be good and render goodness onto others.

This is where the other group comes in to play. To me this group is where you should set your focus. This group has no clue as to who you are or where you're from or what you've been through. This group takes you at face value and will generate their own opinion and engineer by their own bias and have no understanding of what you truly stand for.

This group needs a message, a message that you alone can provide. We all have a Purpose, we all have a reason to be here, and we are all connected. This we should all hold and value as a true statement. This leads us to see one another, it draws us together, and it defines and gives meaning to our lives.

CHAPTER 12

WHERE DOES PURPOSE LEAD US TO OR LEAD US AWAY FROM?

This question is a tough one, because now we must address what "we" want in our lives versus what "we" need in our lives.

Our wants outweigh our needs, is this true? If it's true for you, then, are you living with your Purpose?

I want to be happy, I want to be loved, I want to be successful, I want to live forever – it is safe to say, these are probably the most common desires that we all have. I'm sure there are others that we can debate or discuss and potentially add to this list, but these were the four I decided to focus on.

Everything is relative, I've heard that time and time again and you start to realize, yes, it is, but also, no it is not. So, we will start with happiness. Is there one type of happy? If you asked 100 people to describe or define or explain happiness; would they come back with the same answer? I would venture to say their answers would be similar or have a consistent base. This foundation is what draws us together and these parallels are evident across all spectrums.

To me it is all a test in values, if not this, then that. It is not limited to age, gender or geographic region. I would argue that there are external factors that impact decisions daily that are uncontrolled or may even go unnoticed. Just think, how things impact upon your decisions. Whether you wake up on time or not, whether you are in or not in traffic, whether you eat or don't eat, go to the gym or don't

– the list goes on and on, and we are still in the first part of our day.

So, rewind and start with this thought. Today I will wake up ON Purpose and once I'm awake, I will live WITH Purpose, my Purpose. How does that change your thought process? Where does that drive your thought process? Your decisions would generate different actions and behaviors, would it not?

We need to discuss the "where." Where does my "why" push or lead me to and where does it lead me away from?

Where it leads me, should be directly tied into what specifically it is and what I am directly involved with in my life. Am I driven by my talents? Do my aptitudes allow me to meet and interact with the people I need to meet and with others? Do my abilities serve a greater need or requirement? How do my gifts affect others?

If I am living the right way can I accept that this means I will be led away from people or things that are not on my path? I think we get caught here in this one, for sure. I think that it is our power of "choice" that directly impacts and influences our life, thus it alerts you of all your shortcomings and makes you aware of the quest. It is a "tell" that shouldn't be ignored.

Freedoms are our inalienable rights, that is a phrase that is echoed, and hash tagged, and can probably be seen on a shirt at a rally of some sort. We are entitled, and we not only accept this entitlement, but we expect this entitlement to be respected. How dare you or your group not accept this and who are you not to endorse this opinion?

Sadly, we cannot lose focus as bad as we have recently. We must continue to fight and to pursue with great passion our path while we are here for our moment in time. To live a meaningful life, you must be cognizant and open to things that you value. If we don't think or know or understand that we live but just a fraction in time, then we cannot truly grasp that there are things bigger than us and that will supersede our need to feel different or special.

Where we go is where we grow, why would you not take life on with this phrase. Our where, is defined by us, but it is written by God. Our where is not restricted. Our where can last a long time or can be, but a brief segment in time.

I believe that opportunities are around us and these opportunities do not go unused. They are taken and appreciated by the ones who choose to take them. Irony and coincidence are not truly so farfetched to some but are more defined by others.

You can find it ironic that a chance encounter has been beneficial or even quite the opposite, horrible. This my friend is all a part of your path. There is legitimacy in the phrase, if it was easy, then everyone would do it.

It sounds easy, but many are denied opportunities. Sadly, the one who denies the opportunity is often yourself. You are your own worst enemy, critic or evaluator. You will get in your own way more often than not if you are not focused. Why?

Life can be so chaotic in this complicated world, but the where part should be the fun. Where does life lead me to and where does it lead me away from?

Honestly reflect and answer these two questions, write down your answers, and then reflect again on, is this in line with your principles or what motivates you.

Chapter 13

How Does Our Purpose Drive Us?

Like fuel in a car, our engine in life needs to be driven with meaning. What you wake up to do each morning must be forged in between a position of greatness and a curiosity to acquire knowledge. There are no random events that occur. You're living in a scripted adventured life. You just don't know it yet.

You are meant to grow up in an exact place, go to school in a specific place, meet and interact with certain people. Every interaction has a possibility for enrichment or a variable, if this then that type of equation. One small step, one less second, one changed thought, can impact your course entirely.

I don't think it changes your specific pathway, but it will directly assist you on your time along the route. We must continue to ask ourselves, how does our Purpose drive us today?

Are we motivated even on bad days? Precious is our time here and it is never more evident or apparent than during times of loss. Why do we defer when we are not guaranteed the time we have just literally postponed? We take it for granted because we feel time is an infinite resource that we control.

I remember sitting in the hospital just two months after my mom was diagnosed with cancer listening to her apologize for not making time and choosing work over vacation and time with the grandkids. I had by that time become so immune to loss through multiple deployments, having seen so many go before her, but I was vulnerable in this moment because this loss was more significant.

A mother is to a child, what the horizon is to the sun. There is an artistic beauty in the sunrise, where this great ball of fire and source of light emerges and enlightens the earth daily to complete its purpose within this equation. Mother earth bears the responsibility to receive the sun and to enhance its beauty. What I'm saying is that we are guided by their light and by their love that is unconditional and irreplaceable. You cannot have one without the other and so they are symbiotic in this relationship.

Guilt was the least of my concerns, I was in an exposed state that was unfamiliar. After years of numerous and tragic losses, I sat in a room full of hopelessness knowing that the diagnosis was final. Cancer is an equalizer who has no regard for time or for moments lost or postponed. In that instant I needed something more to focus on besides loss and anger. Because days later, she was gone.

During the days to come, I immediately was enlightened and embraced the authenticity in the following perspective. When you're dead, you can no longer feel the pain of your situation. Others are left to bear the brunt and the weight of that pain, well beyond your physical existence. The finality of death can be disabling to the life that is left to endure this intolerable truth.

> "We need to find God, and He cannot
> be found in noise and restlessness. God is the friend of silence.
> See how nature - trees, flowers, grass- grows in silence; see the
> stars, the moon and the sun, how they move in silence... We
> need silence to be able to touch souls."
> -Mother Teresa

We need to wake up each morning and be deliberate in our actions. We need to get up and begin our day with a specific plan and a goal that drives us forward. We must impact others around us, not only family and friends, but everyone. Do we do that?

When was the last time we helped someone we didn't know? Acts of Random Kindness challenges go around, and they fizzle out, but I think we can really help them grow if we commit to them. If you have a chance, err on the side of kindness.

I learned from my 20 years in service to my country, that you motivate Soldiers simply by two things. You take their time or their money. I don't want that to be or sound as bad as it does in that plain statement. Allow me to explain.

Soldiers are classified as a very diverse and eclectic group, and I had the fortunate opportunity to serve with and lead them throughout my tenured career. I would venture to say that in the civilian sector, time and money dominates and if it's taken away it would create fear or be alarming and attention grabbing.

I will focus on Soldiers or Service Members, one because I was one and can speak to their day-to-day lives and two because they serve as volunteers to a nation that does not truly acknowledge or understand their sacrifices.

If you Google military pay scales, you can easily see what Service Members make in comparison to their civilian counterparts. I would say that money specifically in the Armed Services is not a luxury, but a necessity. Thankfully there are services to assist Soldiers to balance their financial budgets and burdens.

In any career field, you want to be successful and you want to earn your worth. So, you generally will strive for success in your chosen job in hopes of succeeding. Soldiers, unlike their civilian contemporaries, have a distinct difference in their job description. They are there to protect and defend this country from all enemies, foreign and domestic. They are to obey all written laws and orders of the officers appointed over them.

This means that at any time they can be called up and sent off to places unknown for an undisclosed time and therefore "time" is so precious to Soldiers. Time is our most valuable resource anyway, and it should be appreciated no matter what. Because it is one thing that you can give, but it can't be restored. To me, as a retired Soldier now, I can see how my time is spent now and how I cherish my moments more in retirement.

So, when I tell you that time and money dictate what or how you can motivate people, it is from experience. It is not with threats or anything like that. It is just the realization that if you don't do what you need to do and get it done in a timely and efficient manner, then you will stay until it's complete.

The other is self-explanatory, if you think someone is going to mess with your money, suddenly that person has your full attention.

This is an understatement, because we tie so much to money or finances. So the threat, or the loss of any money directly connected to your own action, is not something you want to deal with. You ever wonder why that is the case?

I am certain that this is a learned behavior. We have a set of value systems as well as a set of things we value. It sounds like the same thing, but if you reread that phrase there is a difference between the two.

When you talk about a set of values, what do you think we are talking about? There are values that are taught and learned from an early age. These standards are bestowed upon you by your family and close friends. These morals are tied or linked to things that you would find or consider normal in your life.

There are things we classify. Our values are among the things that get particular attention. What are the things that we value? This would differ from person to person and location to location. The reality is, is that there are things that we enjoy possessing. We appreciate, and we cherish items more than personal relationships. So, each of us have a hierarchy of what is important and naturally, it differs from person to person.

We have identified that there are different standards that we each have, but have we talked about what motivates us to have these ideals. What drives us to pursue our Purpose?

If you think about it, there are a few things that we can look at that drives us towards our, "why." I would like to talk about one. The difference between being complete or being fulfilled would be something I would like to explore further.

What does it mean to be complete? What do we feel when we are fulfilled? These questions required me to think a little bit about what and how we can measure these two.

To be complete can be described as finished or done with a task. When you complete a duty, you've met the requirements laid out for you and confirmed that there was nothing left undone. If you complete a mission does that necessarily equate to you fulfilling the intent of the obligation?

Completion is not fulfillment. What I mean by this, is that even though you complete something you may have not fulfilled and met the actual overall intent. How could this be so? Was your Purpose driving you to completion, if not can you truly feel fulfilled?

I would say that one without the other would not equate to true fulfillment. If you're not being driven and following your reason of existence, you cannot possibly be complete. You need a why, you need to ensure that you're on the track that you are destined to be on. If you don't, then the answer to your equation would be that you cannot truly finish and fulfill your why.

Why Do I Have A Purpose?

This is one you'll have to figure out for yourself. Pull out that paper now, the one I told you to write your Purpose on a few pages back. Now, I ask you to start thinking about your, "why." When you figure out the why, now you must take a moment and honestly think, do I embrace my why?

We all have a talent and we all have a why associated with that God given skill. We must accept and receive our why, not just once, but often. We need to restore, refresh, renew, reinvigorate, and let our why direct our behavior in our daily lives.

> *And we know that in all things God works for the good of those who love Him, who have been called according to His Purpose.*
> -Romans 8:28

My take on the why is that everything needs a direction. They say, *"Not all those who wander are lost,"* a line from the poem, *All that is Gold does not Glitter* written by J. R. R. Tolkien. So, you cannot hit a target without aim or you cannot reach a destination without having waypoints. What is needed is a direction and clarity.

As a junior Soldier, I can remember studying for a promotion board and memorizing the definition of leadership, in my own words because the whole definition was a bit much for me to remember. There were dozens of topics, so you can imagine that there were a lot of things that I summarized.

But, as a student who took to heart what I was learning, I appreciated the shortened definition of leadership. To provide purpose, direction, and motivation to complete the mission. (Army Leadership definition). This was so simple, but so profound to me when I first read through it.

When you take it segment by segment, you really can see that we all are destined to be a leader. In some aspect of your life, you lead. Whether it be yourself or a large group of others, you are still leading and as a leader you need to provide someone with a Purpose. How do you do that? Does everyone have the same Purpose?

There is no cookie cutter method to this that become obvious to me right away. As a leader, you should pride yourself on knowing the people you lead or the people you serve. A servant leader is a successful leader.

Now that you've provided someone with a Purpose, you must give them a direction. This can be difficult at times to translate. Directions are subject to interpretation and you can only guarantee that your message was sent, you just never know how it was received. I sought to be clear and concise when giving a direction.

With a Purpose and a well-articulated direction, you now must offer a motivation. Motivation is defined as, "The reason or reasons one has for acting or behaving in a particular way." The reason you do something is your, "why," so it makes sense that you would need a motivation or a, "need," for that Purpose.

If you combine all of that together it is easy to see while simple and is so true. I truly cherished that well-articulated instruction that led to my accomplishments and the achievements of all the Soldiers I had an opportunity to lead. Giving someone a "WHY" changes their perspective, their insight, and provides meaning on their path.

Ideally, one takes something complex or confusion and makes it clear and transparent which promotes commitment and understanding. You don't know the influence you will have on everyone you interact with, directly or indirectly. You serve and lead daily with your passion and you just never know how that can influence your Soldiers.

I've had a chance to see this influence come full circle in my lifetime. I can list example after example of thoughtful calls or text messages and e-mails that simply say thank you from Service Members that I have led as well as others that were my leaders.

CHAPTER 15

THE PURSUIT OF PURPOSE, WITH PASSION

*"Our deepest fear is not that we are inadequate.
Our deepest fear is that we are powerful beyond measure. It is
our light, not our darkness that most frightens us. We ask
ourselves who am I to be brilliant, gorgeous, talented, fabulous?
Actually, who are you not to be?"*
-Marianne Williamson

How do we pursue our Purpose with passion?

This is the essence of the entire book. This portion of the book looks to complete the movement and place a significance to a worthy message.

Here we are, I've talked about a variety of principles, ideologies and guidelines that I found beneficial throughout my career and life. I've introduced you to a few items that I hope will spur some reflection, some critical thinking and encourage you to evaluate your steps moving forward.

These are all things that I think could help you change the rest of your life. When we discuss the passionate pursuit of Purpose, the secret is, it starts with you. You are the one who determines your effort, you have that choice. You are the one who must recognize and own your strengths and weaknesses. Only you can understand what it is that you are called and chosen to do.

*All these are the work of one and the same Spirit, and He
distributes them to each one, just as He determines.*
-1 Corinthian 12:11

When we talk about the race that you're in, it is a true test of your endurance and your perseverance. It is a persistent self-evaluation that leads you to become a better you. Remember, we are all God's creations and we are here for a precise reason. We are all destined for greatness, this is something that you must know and accept in your heart.

But this road is not the easiest to travel. There will be adversity, there will be trials, there will be loss, there will be chances that you must take, but only you can come to terms and accept your Purpose. This is a huge first step. Identifying your Purpose. Because now that you have done that; what should you do next?

Next is to define, your, "why." When you know and acknowledge your why, you should be led to your passions. This why brings your pursuits full circle. Your why is your confirmation and it is through affirmation within your quests that this is extracted.

The fun part is next, once you acknowledge and accept your why, you must now receive that this is your route and you don't look back. That is a huge step, to commit to something, and walk that trail that you're destined to walk.

Lastly, to me, the thing that brings all of this together is that you must share with others what you have discovered. You have a God given talent or ability, that is yours and it was bestowed upon you by God.

Let that sink in, God gave you something directly. If you don't share it, then you are being self-centered, in my estimation. You should share it with others, you should be ambitious to embark on this journey with others.

> *"Enlightenment is when the wave realizes it is the ocean."*
> -Thich Nhat Hanh

Not all explanations to life will be insightful or profound, but nevertheless, they are yours and you must file them in your memory bank for safe keeping. This life is but a moment, a glimpse in time; do you want to waste it not being intentional? The answer to the question is a resounding NO.

Get out there, join the program that is happening today, right here and right now. I'm Meant To Be Movement is now official, it is here to stay. You are Meant To Be, and now you must get out and inspire others to acknowledge, that they are Meant To Be.

How exciting is this mission and more importantly are you ready to start this endeavor? I encourage you to get out and share this message and then extend yourself out to others and repeat that time and time again. How many other someone else's can this reach? What limitations will you place on yourself? If none, then what boundaries will stop this message? NONE!

Be excited, as I am excited to have given you this message and with total conviction, I charge you to pass it on to others. I leave you with this, enjoy!

You are the light of the world.
A town built on a hill cannot be hidden. Neither do people light a lamp and put it under a bowl. Instead they put it on its stand, and it gives light to everyone in the house. In the same way, let your light shine before others, that they may see your good deeds and glorify your Father in heaven.
-Matthew 5:4-16

◆ ABOUT THE AUTHOR ◆

Alvin King was born in the Lower Eastside of Manhattan and raised in Brooklyn, New York. He is married with two children and after his father's untimely death in 2000, he was granted custody of his younger brother Ryan, whom he raised as well. He now resides in South Carolina upon his retirement from the United States Army. He is a 20-year United States Army Combat Veteran who has had multiple deployments in support of contingency operations all over the world. His reflections and insight are what led him down the path to write this manual that he hopes will prove useful to the reader and spread beyond his reach. His goal is to acquaint others who may benefit from his insight and his experiences and encourage them to accept a very heartfelt message. It is his hope that this message will reach the ones most in need and thereby improve their feelings of self-worth and help them lead a life worth living!

♦ ACKNOWLEDGEMENTS ♦

*All this is for your benefit, so that the grace
that is reaching more and more people may cause thanksgiving to
overflow to the glory of God.*
-2 Corinthians 4:15

First and foremost, I would like to thank God for His Grace, patience and for providing us all with a sense or an example of humility. Without Him all this would certainly not be possible.

Secondly, I would love to thank my wife Dina who has been my rock through all of this. My kids Araesia and Jaelen, and my younger brother Ryan. These four are the reason I do what I do.

To my parents, Alvin and Mary, who have both passed away, I love you and I can only hope that you're looking down sharing in this moment with me. To my step parents Lester and Romaine, I say thank you for being a part of my process and journey. I'm certain that my life was directly influenced and impacted by all of them and for this I remain humble and thankful.

To my "T," Diana, who took on this endeavor with me, I'm forever grateful for your words and your guidance through this process. To my uncle Michael who provided me with two great bookmark poems that captured the spirit of what I discussed. To my Godmother Linda whose unwavering support and encouragement assisted me more than she will ever know. To my older sister Shareen and brother in law Kenny, I thank you for your continued support and guidance you have provided.

Lastly, I would like to thank all my family and friends, Soldiers who I have served with and led, and all that have been a part of my journey. Service members are a collection of our nation's treasures that comprises the less than one percent of the United States that have volunteered to protect and defend the nation and that is sometimes overlooked and undervalued by others. But with one another we will always share a bond that is undeniable and appreciated during the good and the bad times. I want to extend a heartfelt thank you for your service and now as a retired veteran I would like to share my honest, heartfelt and well deserved thank you to those whose currently serve. I'm proud to be here for your continued support. God Bless!

Made in the USA
Columbia, SC
06 August 2022